# Playing the Crusades

*Engaging the Crusades* is a series of volumes which offer windows into a newly emerging field of historical study: the memory and legacy of the crusades. Together these volumes examine the reasons behind the enduring resonance of the crusades and present the memory of crusading in the modern period as a productive, exciting, and much needed area of investigation.

This volume considers the appearance and use of the crusades in modern games; demonstrating that popular memory of the crusades is intrinsically and mutually linked with the design and play of these games. The chapters engage with uses of crusading rhetoric and imagery within a range of genres – including roleplaying, action, strategy, and casual games – and from a variety of theoretical perspectives drawing on gender and race studies, game design and theory, and broader discussions on medievalism. Cumulatively, the authors reveal the complex position of the crusades within digital games, highlight the impact of these games on popular understanding of the crusades, and underline the connection between the portrayal of the crusades in digital games and academic crusade historiography.

*Playing the Crusades* is invaluable for scholars and students interested in the crusades, popular representations of the crusades, historical games, and collective memory.

**Robert Houghton** is Senior Lecturer in Medieval History at the University of Winchester. His research focuses on religious and political relationship networks in the central Middle Ages and on representations of the medieval world in modern games. Recent publications include 'Italian Bishops and Warfare during the Investiture Contest: The Case of Parma' (2018) and 'World, Structure and Play: Digital Games as Historical Research Tools' (2018).

# ENGAGING THE CRUSADES

THE MEMORY AND LEGACY THE CRUSADES

SERIES EDITORS
JONATHAN PHILLIPS & MIKE HORSWELL

# Engaging the Crusades
The Memory and Legacy of Crusading
Series Editors: Jonathan Phillips and Mike Horswell
Royal Holloway
*University of London, UK.*

*Engaging the Crusades* is a series of volumes which offer initial windows into the ways in which the crusades have been used in the last two centuries; demonstrating that the memory of the crusades is an important and emerging subject. Together these studies suggest that the memory of the crusades, in the modern period, is a productive, exciting and much needed area of investigation.

In this series:

**Perceptions of the Crusades from the Nineteenth to the Twenty-First Century**
Engaging the Crusades, Volume One
*Edited by Jonathan Phillips and Mike Horswell*

**The Crusades in the Modern World**
Engaging the Crusades, Volume Two
*Edited by Mike Horswell and Akil N. Awan*

**Controversial Histories – Current Views on the Crusades**
Engaging the Crusades, Volume Three
*Edited by Felix Hinz and Johannes Meyer-Hamme*

**The Making of Crusading Heroes and Villains**
Engaging the Crusades, Volume Four
*Edited by Mike Horswell and Kristin Skottki*

**Playing the Crusades**
Engaging the Crusades, Volume Five
*Edited by Robert Houghton*

For more information about this series, please visit: www.routledge.com/Engaging-the-Crusades/book-series/ETC

# Playing the Crusades
Engaging the Crusades,
Volume Five

**Edited by Robert Houghton**

LONDON AND NEW YORK

First published 2021
by Routledge
2 Park Square, Milton Park, Abingdon, Oxon OX14 4RN

and by Routledge
52 Vanderbilt Avenue, New York, NY 10017

*Routledge is an imprint of the Taylor & Francis Group, an informa business*

© 2021 selection and editorial matter, Robert Houghton; individual chapters, the contributors

The right of Robert Houghton to be identified as the author of the editorial material, and of the authors for their individual chapters, has been asserted in accordance with sections 77 and 78 of the Copyright, Designs and Patents Act 1988.

All rights reserved. No part of this book may be reprinted or reproduced or utilised in any form or by any electronic, mechanical, or other means, now known or hereafter invented, including photocopying and recording, or in any information storage or retrieval system, without permission in writing from the publishers.

*Trademark notice*: Product or corporate names may be trademarks or registered trademarks, and are used only for identification and explanation without intent to infringe.

*British Library Cataloguing-in-Publication Data*
A catalogue record for this book is available from the British Library

*Library of Congress Cataloging-in-Publication Data*
A catalog record for this book has been requested

ISBN: 978-0-367-26441-3 (hbk)
ISBN: 978-0-367-71635-6 (pbk)
ISBN: 978-0-429-29326-9 (ebk)

Typeset in Times New Roman
by Apex CoVantage, LLC

# Contents

*List of contributors* viii
*Acknowledgements* x

Introduction: crusades and crusading in modern games 1
ROBERT HOUGHTON

1 A sacred task, no cross required: the image of crusading in computer gaming-related non-Christian science fiction universes 12
ROLAND WENSKUS

2 'I'm not responsible for the man you are!': crusading and masculinities in *Dante's Inferno* 30
KATHERINE J. LEWIS

3 'Show this fool knight what it is to have no fear': freedom and oppression in *Assassin's Creed* (2007) 53
OANA-ALEXANDRA CHIRILĂ

4 Crusader kings too? (Mis)Representations of the crusades in strategy games 71
ROBERT HOUGHTON

5 Learning to think historically: some theoretical challenges when playing the crusades 93
ANDREAS KÖRBER, JOHANNES MEYER-HAMME, AND ROBERT HOUGHTON

*Index* 111

# Contributors

**Oana-Alexandra Chirilă** is a PhD student in Literary and Cultural Studies at the University of Bucharest, Romania, and an avid video gamer. She has published several articles and lectured at both national and international conferences and symposiums. Oana's main academic interests focus around views on psychoactive substances in Islam. Most recently, she has completed a Fulbright Student Award grant as Junior Researcher at Lehigh University, PA. Oana is scheduled to defend her doctoral thesis, *Intoxicants in Black Islamic American Hip Hop*, in the spring of 2021.

**Robert Houghton** is Senior Lecturer in Early Medieval History at the University of Winchester. His current research addresses two key themes: political networks in the central Middle Ages and the representation of the Middle Ages in Modern Games. His recent articles include 'Hugh, Lothar and Berengar: The Balance of Power in Italy 945–950' (2020) and 'World, Structure and Play: Digital Games as Historical Research Tools' (2018). He is currently preparing a monograph titled *The Middle Ages in Modern Games: Approaches to the Medieval and Medievalism*.

**Andreas Körber** is Professor of Education, History and Political Science Education at Hamburg University. His research focuses on historical thinking and learning, intercultural and inclusive history education, history and memory cultures, and public history. His recent articles include 'Geschichte – Spielen – Denken. Kontingenzverschiebungen und zweiseitige Triftigkeiten' (2018) and 'Translation and its Discontents II: A German Perspective' (2016).

**Katherine J. Lewis** is Senior Lecturer in History at the University of Huddersfield. Her research focuses on medieval gender identities and their construction in both medieval and modern narratives. Her publications include *Kingship and Masculinity in Late Medieval England* (2013), and she is co-editor of *Crusading and Masculinities* (2019). She has also published on the cults of female saints, especially St Katherine of Alexandria, and The Book of Margery Kempe.

**Johannes Meyer-Hamme** is Professor of Theory and Didactics of History at the University of Paderborn. His research focuses on questions of historical theory and theories of historical learning, especially with regard to social heterogeneity, as well as on empirical research on historical awareness in society and competencies of historical thinking with qualitative and quantitative methods. His recent publications include 'The Tension Between Historical Thinking and Historical Culture' (2019) and he co-edited *Controversial Histories – Current Views on the Crusades* (*Engaging the Crusades, Volume Three*, 2020).

**Roland Wenskus** is currently working on his PhD thesis at the University of Saarbrücken. His main areas of interest include chivalry and chivalric concepts, the crusades, the reception of medieval imagery in popular culture, and the history of the Armed Services of the former German Democratic Republic.

# Acknowledgements

I would like to thank all of the contributors to this volume for their ceaseless work and extensive patience. Their pieces approach the crusades and modern games from diverse and innovative perspectives and methodologies and have greatly contributed to my understanding of this emergent theme. Thanks also go to Morwenna Scott and Isabel Voice at Routledge for guiding this book to publication through very difficult events. I also need to thank Mike Horswell for his acceptance of the volume into the *Engaging the Crusades* series and for all his help throughout its production. Finally, I want to thank Varan for her support, humour, and friendship.

# Introduction
## Crusades and crusading in modern games

*Robert Houghton*

The crusades are used frequently and extensively as source material for digital games. The first of the *Assassin's Creed* series with its free-running action across the cities of the Middle East during the Third Crusade is perhaps the best-known, and best-selling, example, but modern representations of the crusades are influential across almost every genre. Real-time Strategy Games such as *Stronghold: Crusader* or *Age of Empires II* explore the characters and events of the crusades in a fairly simple and linear manner.[1] The crusades are key to the world building of roleplaying games (RPG) such as *Lionheart: Legacy of the Crusader* or *Legacy of Kain* but their reach extends to almost every RPG presentation of Western 'holy warriors' from the Crusaders of *Diablo III* and the Templars of *Elder Scrolls Online* to the Paladins ubiquitous to *World of Warcraft, Final Fantasy*, and a host of games which draw on the *Dungeons and Dragons* ruleset. Grand Strategy Games such as *Civilization, Medieval: Total War*, or *Crusader Kings* almost invariably incorporate the crusades into their complex explorations of medieval politics and society.[2]

The use of the crusades, and the Middle Ages more generally, in digital games in this manner has influenced public perceptions in several ways. These games have introduced a vast and largely untapped audience to this period of history.[3] They have underlined the fact that the Middle Ages did not end at the boundaries of Europe, and highlighted that armoured knights and elaborate castles existed within an intricate and diverse wider world.[4] They have acted as educational tools at several levels of study.[5] Ultimately, they have provided a new historical approach to the crusades which is of interest and utility to students, academics, and the wider world.

However, these games almost never provide a coherent or thorough explanation and examination of the crusades. There is a tendency towards simplification of very complex events into simple binary conflicts between Christians and Muslims.[6] Gameplay is typically Eurocentric, producing a skewed perspective of the period with non-Christian and non-white characters and groups relegated to a supporting role.[7] A focus on violence and warfare (which is comparatively easy to model, and which often helps to sell games)[8] robs many games of nuance. The historical research which supports the creation of these games is sometimes based on outdated works, unreliable websites, or popular misconceptions.[9] Many games lean more heavily on medieval and modern fictions about the period than on modern academic historical research.[10] Creation of enjoyable gameplay and catering to audience expectations frequently overshadows any attempts at 'historical accuracy'.[11]

Historical misrepresentations within games are problematic because these media can exert a substantial influence over their players' understanding of the past both inside and outwith the classroom.[12] The potential of digital games as historical learning and communication tools is powerful and increasingly recognised within academic and industry circles.[13] Games can address important issues in a mature and considered manner.[14] They can present complex stories through innovative and diverse methods.[15] Games with a historical setting or themes can engage their players with the past, introducing them to new periods and issues and providing a formative understanding of events and underlying trends.[16] As Bogost has demonstrated, the procedural rhetoric by which games construct and express their arguments can be immensely compelling and can dramatically influence players' perspectives.[17] This interactive engagement often represents the deepest interaction a player has with the past,[18] and this is particularly true in relation to pre-modern periods.[19] As a result, games can be powerful educational tools. They can act as an entry point to specific periods and events or to historical themes.[20] They can be used to teach historical theory through their mechanics.[21] By engaging with these mechanics through play and modification, students may conduct historical debate, create counterarguments and develop a more nuanced understanding of the past.[22] There is even potential to use games as academic research tools, communicating historical data and arguments and facilitating debate.[23]

However, the potency of games as influencing media can easily lead to their audiences obtaining fundamentally incomplete, shallow or misleading impressions about the crusades and the Middle Ages more generally.[24] This can be an issue within the history classroom as this often deeply embedded formative understanding can be hard to reconcile with the course content, primary sources, and historiographical trends and increasingly requires teachers to be aware of themes and representations within modern games.[25]

Beyond the classroom, the potent influencing capabilities of digital games can severely colour their players' understanding of the past.[26] This becomes an issue when a game's representation of a period takes on the form of harmful modern perceptions and ideologies. Strategy games frequently follow an acritical model of colonialism and imperialism which emphasises violent expansionism as the core driver of civilisation and whitewashes the human and cultural consequences of these political models.[27] The focus on white male characters and emphasis on violence within many historical digital games,[28] in combination with their claimed authority,[29] can easily lead to the emergence and consolidation of a distorted view of the period which can contribute to racist and misogynist understandings of the modern world: the presentation of the Middle Ages and other historical periods as White feeds into the expectations of extremist and mainstream players and goes unchallenged by acritical design studios.[30] Historical accuracy is often cited as the reason for a lack of diversity in images of the Middle Ages presented by games and other modern media, but in many cases this accuracy is selective and incomplete and serves only to reinforce the perspectives and prejudices of the core audience.[31]

The use of the crusades and crusading tropes within and around digital games is an important battleground within this ideological conflict. Crusade rhetoric has been deployed consistently by right-wing groups across media formats to support their modern ideologies of racial and religious purity and the need to protect their pure nation from outsiders.[32] The same rhetoric has been embraced by Islamic extremists in support of their campaigns against the West.[33] Beyond this, within popular imagination and political rhetoric the crusades are closely connected to the ideologies of colonialism, imperialism, and racial and religious violence.[34] These popular visualisations of the crusades correspond closely to the various issues common within digital games in general. As a result, games about the crusades can easily support some of the most extreme ideologies.

This is not to say that representations of the crusades in all digital games are inevitably and absolutely problematic. While many games present overly simplistic visualisations which lean on outdated viewpoints and troubling ideologies, even these limited representations can be of educational use when approached critically.[35] Counter-play and user-modification may replace or challenge many of these Eurocentric perspectives with more balanced approaches.[36] Beyond this, several games which address the crusades provide nuanced and thoughtful elements within their core narrative and mechanics, even if they retain some troublesome elements. For example, *Assassin's Creed* presents a non-Western viewpoint through its player character while *Crusader Kings II* provides a relatively detailed and nuanced representation of the medieval Middle East even if it occasionally relies on outdated viewpoints and stereotypes. Other games, such as *Dante's Inferno*, make use of tropes and misconceptions about the crusades to engage with modern ideas and issues in constructive ways. Ultimately, as is the case with historical representations in games more generally, the issue is the presentation of historical content in certain games rather than the fundamental characteristics of the medium.[37]

This book draws together several strands and themes surrounding the representation of the crusades within digital games. Roland Wenskaus' chapter highlights the presence of crusading tropes in games within both the fantasy and science fiction genres to demonstrate that the influence of the crusades and their attendant literature stretches well beyond historical games. In her chapter, Katherine J. Lewis discusses the portrayal of crusader masculinity within *Dante's Inferno* and considers the adaption of these medieval masculinities for a modern audience. Oana-Alexandra Chirilă's article draws on the widespread and ongoing discussion of the representation of the Islamic world in modern games to provide a focused and in-depth analysis of the potential to develop a more holistic and balanced ludic vision. Robert Houghton discusses the restrictions of game mechanics and player expectations which limit the exploration of the political and social development of the crusades within strategy games and suggests some practical solutions to these issues. In the final chapter Andreas Körber, Johannes Meyer-Hamme, and Robert Houghton address the potential of digital games as learning and teaching tools for the study of the crusades.

Taken as a whole, these chapters provide a diverse but coherent exploration of the place of the crusades within games and the opportunities posed by this media form for greater engagement with and discussion of this theme. This volume is by no means encyclopaedic, but represents an important starting point for the subject.

## Notes

1 Vit Šisler, "From Kuma\War to Quraish: Representation of Islam in Arab and American Video Games," in *Playing with Religion in Digital Games*, ed. Heidi Campbell and Gregory P. Grieve, Digital Game Studies (Bloomington, IN: Indiana University Press, 2014), 120–23.
2 Tom Apperley, "Modding the Historians Code: Historical Versimilitude and the Counterfactual Imagination," in *Playing with the Past: Digital Games and the Simulation of History*, ed. Matthew Kapell and Andrew B. R. Elliott (New York, NY: Bloomsbury, 2013), 185–98; Rolfe Daus Peterson, Andrew Justin Miller, and Sean Joseph Fedorko, "The Same River Twice: Exploring Historical Representation and the Value of Simulation in the Total War, Civilization and Patrician Franchises," in *Playing with the Past: Digital Games and the Simulation of History*, ed. Matthew Kapell and Andrew B. R. Elliott (New York, NY: Bloomsbury, 2013), 41–43.
3 Robert Houghton, "Where Did You Learn That? The Self-Perceived Educational Impact of Historical Computer Games on Undergraduates," *Gamevironments* 5 (2016): 26.

Introduction 5

4 Mirt Komel, "Orientalism in Assassin's Creed: Self-Orientalizing the Assassins from Forerunners of Modern Terrorism into Occidentalized Heroes," *Teorija in Praksa* 51 (2014): 72–90.
5 Jeremiah McCall, "Teaching History With Digital Historical Games: An Introduction to the Field and Best Practices," *Simulation & Gaming* 47, no. 4 (August 1, 2016): 526; Mike Horswell, "Historicising *Assassin's Creed*: Crusader Medievalism, Historiography and Digital Games," in *Teaching the Middle Ages through Modern Games: Using, Modding and Creating Games for Education and Impact*, ed. Robert Houghton (Amsterdam: ARC Humanities Press, Forthcoming).
6 Šisler, "From Kuma\War to Quraish," 109.
7 Komel, "Orientalism in Assassin's Creed."
8 Ernest Adams, *Fundamentals of Game Design*, 3rd ed., Voices That Matter (Berkeley, CA: New Riders, 2014), 423.
9 Tom Taylor, "Historical Simulations and the Future of the Historical Narrative," *History and Computing* 6, no. 2 (2003); Jeremiah McCall, "Video Games as Participatory Public History," in *A Companion to Public History*, ed. D. M. Dean (Hoboken, NJ: Wiley, 2018), 406–7.
10 Oliver M. Traxel, "Medieval and Pseudo-Medieval Elements in Computer Role-Playing Games: Use and Interactivity," in *Medievalism in Technology Old and New*, ed. Karl Fugelso and Carol L. Robinson, Studies in Medievalism 16 (Cambridge and Rochester, NY: D.S. Brewer, 2008), 125.
11 Jesper Juul, *Half-Real: Video Games between Real Rules and Fictional Worlds* (Cambridge, MA: MIT Press, 2005), 19–20; Josef Köstlbauer, "Do Computers Play History?" in *Early Modernity and Video Games*, ed. Tobias Winnerling and Florian Kerschbaumer (Newcastle: Cambridge Scholars, 2014), 25–26; Stefan Donecker, "Pharaoh Mao Zedong and the Musketeers of Babylon: The Civilization Series between Primordialist Nationalism and Subversive Parody," in *Early Modernity and Video Games*, ed. Tobias Winnerling and Florian Kerschbaumer (Newcastle: Cambridge Scholars, 2014), 116.
12 Houghton, "Where Did You Learn That?" 24–25; Jeremiah McCall, "Playing with the Past: History and Video Games (and Why It Might Matter)," *Journal of Geek Studies* 6, no. 1 (2019): 38–39.
13 Walter Oppenheim, "Complex Games and Simulations in Schools," *Teaching History* 34 (1982): 26; Andrew McMichael, "PC Games and the Teaching of History," *The History Teacher* 40, no. 2 (2007): 203–18; Sean Gouglas et al., "Abort, Retry, Pass, Fail: Games as Teaching Tools," in *Pastplay: Teaching and Learning History with Technology*, ed. Kevin Kee (Ann Arbor, MI: University of Michigan Press, 2014), 121–38; McCall, "Teaching History With Digital Historical Games."
14 Adam Chapman, "Is Sid Meier's Civilization History?" *Rethinking History* 17, no. 3 (2013): 313.
15 Dawn Spring, "Gaming History: Computer and Video Games as Historical Scholarship," *Rethinking History* 19, no. 2 (2015): 218.
16 Oppenheim, "Complex Games and Simulations in Schools," 26; Mary Flanagan, *Critical Play: Radical Game Design* (Cambridge, MA: MIT Press, 2013); Jerome De Groot, *Consuming History: Historians and Heritage in Contemporary Popular Culture*, 2nd ed. (London: Taylor & Francis Group, 2016), 152.
17 Ian Bogost, "The Rhetoric of Video Games," in *The Ecology of Games: Connecting Youth, Games, and Learning*, ed. Katie Salen Tekinbaş, The John D.

and Catherine T. Macarthur Foundation Series on Digital Media and Learning (Cambridge, MA: MIT Press, 2008), 117–40; Ian Bogost, *Persuasive Games: The Expressive Power of Videogames* (Cambridge, MA: MIT Press, 2010).
18 Jerremie Clyde, Howard Hopkins, and Glenn Wilkinson, "Beyond the 'Historical' Simulation: Using Theories of History to Inform Scholarly Game Design," *Loading . . . The Journal of the Canadian Game Studies Association* 6, no. 9 (2012): 6; Chapman, "Is Sid Meier's Civilization History?"
19 Houghton, "Where Did You Learn That?" 25–26.
20 Richard Levy and Peter Dawson, "Interactive Worlds as Educational Tools for Understanding Arctic Life," in *Pastplay: Teaching and Learning History with Technology*, ed. Kevin Kee (Ann Arbor, MI: University of Michigan Press, 2014), 66–86; Matthew Nicholls, "Digital Visualisation in Classics Teaching and Beyond," *Journal of Classics Teaching* 17, no. 33 (2016): 27–30.
21 Taylor, "Historical Simulations"; Clyde et al., "Beyond the 'Historical' Simulation," 49; Chapman, "Is Sid Meier's Civilization History?" 315–16; A. Martin Wainwright, "Teaching Historical Theory through Video Games," *The History Teacher* 47, no. 4 (2014): 583; Adam Chapman, *Digital Games as History: How Videogames Represent the Past and Offer Access to Historical Practice*, Routledge Advances in Game Studies 7 (New York, NY: Routledge, 2016), 253–56.
22 Shawn Graham, "Rolling Your Own: On Modding Commercial Games for Educational Goals," in *Pastplay: Teaching and Learning History with Technology*, ed. Kevin Kee (Ann Arbor, MI: University of Michigan Press, 2014), 226–27; Kee, *Pastplay*, 278–79; Wainwright, "Teaching Historical Theory through Video Games," 579; Andrew B. R. Elliott, "Simulations and Simulacra: History in Video Games," *Práticas Da História* 5 (2017): 11–41.
23 Clyde et al., "Beyond the 'Historical' Simulation"; Jeremy Antley, "Going Beyond the Textual in History," *Journal of Digital Humanities* 1, no. 2 (2012); Spring, "Gaming History"; Vinicius Marino Carvalho, "Videogames as Tools for Social Science History," *Historian* 79, no. 4 (2017): 794–819; Robert Houghton, "World, Structure and Play: A Framework for Games as Historical Research Outputs, Tools, and Processes," *Práticas Da História* 7 (2018): 11–43; Robert Houghton, "Scholarly History through Digital Games: Pedagogical Practice as Research Method," *The Interactive Pasts* 2 (2020).
24 Jeremy Antley, "Period Piece: Board Games Can Manipulate Players by Manipulating History," *Real Life* [blog], November 12, 2018, http://reallifemag.com/period-piece/, accessed August 12, 2019.
25 Houghton, "Where Did You Learn That?" 32; McCall, "Playing with the Past," 46.
26 Houghton, "Where Did You Learn That?" 24–25; Sian Beavers, "The Informal Learning of History with Digital Games" (PhD diss., Open University, 2019), 78–80.
27 Souvik Mukherjee, "Playing Subaltern: Video Games and Postcolonialism," *Games and Culture* 13, no. 5 (July 2018): 506–7; Sybille Lammes and Stephanie de Smale, "Hybridity, Reflexivity and Mapping: A Collaborative Ethnography of Postcolonial Gameplay," *Open Library of Humanities* 4, no. 1 (2018): 7; Souvik Mukherjee and Emil Lundedal Hammar, "Introduction to the Special Issue on Postcolonial Perspectives in Game Studies," *Open Library of Humanities* 4, no. 2 (2018): 2; Rhett Loban and Tom Apperley, "Eurocentric Values at Play: Modding the Colonial from the Indigenous Perspective," in *Video Games*

*and the Global South*, ed. Phillip Penix-Tadsen (Pittsburgh, PA: Carnegie Mellon University, 2019), 89.
28 D. Williams et al., "The Virtual Census: Representations of Gender, Race and Age in Video Games," *New Media & Society* 11, no. 5 (2009): 815–34; Lisa Nakamura, "Queer Female of Color: The Highest Difficulty Setting There Is? Gaming Rhetoric as Gender Capital," *ADA* 1 (2012), https://doi.org/10.7264/N37P8W9V, accessed November 12, 2016; Emil Lundedal Hammar, "Counter-Hegemonic Commemorative Play: Marginalized Pasts and the Politics of Memory in the Digital Game Assassin's Creed: Freedom Cry," *Rethinking History* 21, no. 3 (2017): 372–95; Hanli Geyser, "Decolonising the Games Curriculum: Interventions in an Introductory Game Design Course," *Open Library of Humanities* 4, no. 1 (2018): 33.
29 Scott Alan Metzger and Richard J. Paxton, "Gaming History: A Framework for What Video Games Teach About the Past," *Theory & Research in Social Education* 44, no. 4 (2016): 550–53.
30 Jessie Daniels and Nick Lalone, "Racism in Video Gaming: Connecting Extremist and Mainstream Expressions of White Supremacy," in *Social Exclusion, Power, and Video Game Play: New Research in Digital Media and Technology*, ed. David G. Embrick, J. Talmadge Wright, and András Lukács (Lanham, MD: Lexington Books, 2012), 85–100.
31 Helen Young, "Whiteness and Time: The Once, Present and Future Race," in *Medievalism on the Margins*, ed. Karl Fugelso, Vincent Ferré, and Alicia C. Montoya, Studies in Medievalism 24 (Cambridge: Boydell and Brewer, 2015), 44–45; Andrew B. R. Elliott, *Medievalism, Politics and Mass Media: Appropriating the Middle Ages in the Twenty-First Century*, Medievalism, Vol. 10 (Woodbridge: D. S. Brewer, 2017), 155–82.
32 Vít Šisler, "Digital Arabs: Representation in Video Games," *European Journal of Cultural Studies* 11, no. 2 (2008): 208–10; Elliott, *Medievalism, Politics and Mass Media*, 78–105.
33 Elliott, *Medievalism, Politics and Mass Media*, 106–31.
34 Joshua Prawer, *The Crusaders' Kingdom: European Colonialism in the Middle Ages* (London: Phoenix Press, 2001), 60; Ronnie Ellenblum, *Crusader Castles and Modern Histories* (Cambridge: Cambridge University Press, 2007), 18–31, 43–49; Christopher Tyerman, *The Debate on the Crusades*, Issues in Historiography (Manchester: Manchester University Press, 2011), 125–54; Elliott, *Medievalism, Politics and Mass Media*, 132–54.
35 Kevin Schut, "Strategic Simulations and Our Past: The Bias of Computer Games in the Presentation of History," *Games and Culture* 2, no. 3 (2007): 231; Patrick Crogan, *Gameplay Mode: War, Simulation, and Technoculture*, Electronic Mediations 36 (Minneapolis, MN: University of Minnesota Press, 2011), 174–75; Wainwright, "Teaching Historical Theory through Video Games"; McCall, "Teaching History With Digital Historical Games," 534.
36 Tom Apperley, *Gaming Rhythms: Play and Counterplay from the Situated to the Global* (Amsterdam: Institute of Network Cultures, 2009), 135; Nick Dyer-Witheford and Greig De Peuter, *Games of Empire: Global Capitalism and Video Games*, Electronic Mediations 29 (Minneapolis, MN, 2009), 191–94; Chapman, *Digital Games as History*, 38–39.
37 Jeremiah McCall, "Navigating the Problem Space: The Medium of Simulation Games in the Teaching of History," *History Teacher* 1 (2012): 19–21.

## Bibliography

Adams, Ernest. *Fundamentals of Game Design.* 3rd ed. Voices That Matter. Berkeley, CA: New Riders, 2014.

Antley, Jeremy. "Going Beyond the Textual in History." *Journal of Digital Humanities* 1, no. 2 (2012).

———. "Period Piece: Board Games Can Manipulate Players by Manipulating History." *Real Life* [blog], November 12, 2018. http://reallifemag.com/period-piece/. Accessed August 12, 2019.

Apperley, Tom. *Gaming Rhythms: Play and Counterplay from the Situated to the Global.* Amsterdam: Institute of Network Cultures, 2009.

———. "Modding the Historians Code: Historical Versimilitude and the Counterfactual Imagination." In *Playing with the Past: Digital Games and the Simulation of History*, edited by Matthew Kapell and Andrew B. R. Elliott, 185–98. New York, NY: Bloomsbury, 2013.

Beavers, Sian. "The Informal Learning of History with Digital Games." PhD thesis, Open University, 2019.

Bogost, Ian. *Persuasive Games: The Expressive Power of Videogames.* Cambridge, MA: MIT Press, 2010.

———. "The Rhetoric of Video Games." In *The Ecology of Games: Connecting Youth, Games, and Learning*, edited by Katie Salen Tekinbaş. The John D. and Catherine T. Macarthur, 117–40. Foundation Series on Digital Media and Learning. Cambridge, MA: MIT Press, 2008.

Carvalho, Vinicius Marino. "Videogames as Tools for Social Science History." *Historian* 79, no. 4 (December 2017): 794–819.

Chapman, Adam. *Digital Games as History: How Videogames Represent the Past and Offer Access to Historical Practice.* Routledge Advances in Game Studies 7. New York, NY: Routledge, 2016.

———. "Is Sid Meier's Civilization History?" *Rethinking History* 17, no. 3 (September 2013): 312–32.

Clyde, Jerremie, Howard Hopkins, and Glenn Wilkinson. "Beyond the 'Historical' Simulation: Using Theories of History to Inform Scholarly Game Design." *Loading . . . The Journal of the Canadian Game Studies Association* 6, no. 9 (2012).

Crogan, Patrick. *Gameplay Mode: War, Simulation, and Technoculture.* Electronic Mediations 36. Minneapolis, MN: University of Minnesota Press, 2011.

Daniels, Jessie, and Nick Lalone. "Racism in Video Gaming: Connecting Extremist and Mainstream Expressions of White Supremacy." In *Social Exclusion, Power, and Video Game Play: New Research in Digital Media and Technology*, edited by David G. Embrick, J. Talmadge Wright, and András Lukács, 85–100. Lanham, MD: Lexington Books, 2012.

De Groot, Jerome. *Consuming History: Historians and Heritage in Contemporary Popular Culture.* 2nd ed. London: Taylor & Francis Group, 2016.

Donecker, Stefan. "Pharaoh Mao Zedong and the Musketeers of Babylon: The Civilization Series between Primordialist Nationalism and Subversive Parody."

In *Early Modernity and Video Games*, edited by Tobias Winnerling and Florian Kerschbaumer, 105–22. Newcastle: Cambridge Scholars, 2014.

Dyer-Witheford, Nick, and Greig De Peuter. *Games of Empire: Global Capitalism and Video Games*. Electronic Mediations 29. Minneapolis, MN: University of Minnesota Press, 2009.

Ellenblum, Ronnie. *Crusader Castles and Modern Histories*. Cambridge: Cambridge University Press, 2007.

Elliott, Andrew B. R. *Medievalism, Politics and Mass Media: Appropriating the Middle Ages in the Twenty-First Century*. Medievalism, Vol. 10. Woodbridge: D. S. Brewer, 2017.

———. "Simulations and Simulacra: History in Video Games." *Práticas Da História* 5 (2017): 11–41.

Flanagan, Mary. *Critical Play: Radical Game Design*. Cambridge, MA: MIT Press, 2013.

Geyser, Hanli. "Decolonising the Games Curriculum: Interventions in an Introductory Game Design Course." *Open Library of Humanities* 4, no. 1 (June 11, 2018): 33.

Gouglas, Sean, Mihaela Ilovan, Shannon Lucky, and Silvia Russell. "Abort, Retry, Pass, Fail: Games as Teaching Tools." In *Pastplay: Teaching and Learning History with Technology*, edited by Kevin Kee, 121–38. Ann Arbor, MI: University of Michigan Press, 2014.

Graham, Shawn. "Rolling Your Own: On Modding Commercial Games for Educational Goals." In *Pastplay: Teaching and Learning History with Technology*, edited by Kevin Kee, 214–27. Ann Arbor, MI: University of Michigan Press, 2014.

Hammar, Emil Lundedal. "Counter-Hegemonic Commemorative Play: Marginalized Pasts and the Politics of Memory in the Digital Game Assassin's Creed: Freedom Cry." *Rethinking History* 21, no. 3 (2017): 372–95.

Horswell, Mike. "Historicising *Assassin's Creed*: Crusader Medievalism, Historiography and Digital Games." In *Teaching the Middle Ages through Modern Games: Using, Modding and Creating Games for Education and Impact*, edited by Robert Houghton. Amsterdam: ARC Humanities Press, Forthcoming.

Houghton, Robert. "Scholarly History through Digital Games: Pedagogical Practice as Research Method." *The Interactive Pasts* 2 (2020).

———. "Where Did You Learn That? The Self-Perceived Educational Impact of Historical Computer Games on Undergraduates." *Gamevironments* 5 (2016): 8–45.

———. "World, Structure and Play: A Framework for Games as Historical Research Outputs, Tools, and Processes." *Práticas Da História* 7 (2018): 11–43.

Juul, Jesper. *Half-Real: Video Games between Real Rules and Fictional Worlds*. Cambridge, MA: MIT Press, 2005.

Kee, Kevin, ed. *Pastplay: Teaching and Learning History with Technology*. Ann Arbor, MI: University of Michigan Press, 2014.

Komel, Mirt. "Orientalism in Assassin's Creed: Self-Orientalizing the Assassins from Forerunners of Modern Terrorism into Occidentalized Heroes." *Teorija in Praska* 51 (2014): 72–90.

Köstlbauer, Josef. "Do Computers Play History?" In *Early Modernity and Video Games*, edited by Tobias Winnerling and Florian Kerschbaumer, 24–37. Newcastle: Cambridge Scholars, 2014.

Lammes, Sybille, and Stephanie de Smale. "Hybridity, Reflexivity and Mapping: A Collaborative Ethnography of Postcolonial Gameplay." *Open Library of Humanities* 4, no. 1 (2018): 19.

Levy, Richard, and Peter Dawson. "Interactive Worlds as Educational Tools for Understanding Arctic Life." In *Pastplay: Teaching and Learning History with Technology*, edited by Kevin Kee, 66–86. Ann Arbor, MI: University of Michigan Press, 2014.

Loban, Rhett, and Tom Apperley. "Eurocentric Values at Play: Modding the Colonial from the Indigenous Perspective." In *Video Games and the Global South*, edited by Phillip Penix-Tadsen, 87–99. Pittsburgh, PA: Carnegie Mellon University, 2019.

McCall, Jeremiah. "Navigating the Problem Space: The Medium of Simulation Games in the Teaching of History." *History Teacher* 1 (2012): 9–28.

———. "Playing with the Past: History and Video Games (and Why It Might Matter)." *Journal of Geek Studies* 6, no. 1 (2019): 29–48.

———. "Teaching History with Digital Historical Games: An Introduction to the Field and Best Practices." *Simulation & Gaming* 47, no. 4 (2016): 517–42.

———. "Video Games as Participatory Public History." In *A Companion to Public History*, edited by D. M. Dean, 405–16. Hoboken, NJ: Wiley, 2018.

McMichael, Andrew. "PC Games and the Teaching of History." *The History Teacher* 40, no. 2 (2007): 203–18.

Metzger, Scott Alan, and Richard J. Paxton. "Gaming History: A Framework for What Video Games Teach About the Past." *Theory & Research in Social Education* 44, no. 4 (2016): 532–64.

Mukherjee, Souvik. "Playing Subaltern: Video Games and Postcolonialism." *Games and Culture* 13, no. 5 (2018): 504–20.

Mukherjee, Souvik, and Emil Lundedal Hammar. "Introduction to the Special Issue on Postcolonial Perspectives in Game Studies." *Open Library of Humanities* 4, no. 2 (November 6, 2018): 1–33.

Nakamura, Lisa. "Queer Female of Color: The Highest Difficulty Setting There Is? Gaming Rhetoric as Gender Capital." *ADA* 1 (2012). https://doi.org/10.7264/N37P8W9V. Accessed November 12, 2016.

Nicholls, Matthew. "Digital Visualisation in Classics Teaching and Beyond." *Journal of Classics Teaching* 17, no. 33 (2016): 27–30.

Oppenheim, Walter. "Complex Games and Simulations in Schools." *Teaching History* no. 34 (1982): 26–27.

Peterson, Rolfe Daus, Andrew Justin Miller, and Sean Joseph Fedorko. "The Same River Twice: Exploring Historical Representation and the Value of Simulation in the Total War, Civilization and Patrician Franchises." In *Playing with the Past: Digital Games and the Simulation of History*, edited by Matthew Kapell and Andrew B. R. Elliott, 33–48. New York, NY: Bloomsbury, 2013.

Prawer, Joshua. *The Crusaders' Kingdom: European Colonialism in the Middle Ages*. London: Phoenix Press, 2001.

Schut, Kevin. "Strategic Simulations and Our Past: The Bias of Computer Games in the Presentation of History." *Games and Culture* 2, no. 3 (2007): 213–35.
Šisler, Vít. "Digital Arabs: Representation in Video Games." *European Journal of Cultural Studies* 11, no. 2 (May 2008): 203–20.
Šisler, Vít. "From Kuma\War to Quraish: Representation of Islam in Arab and American Video Games." In *Playing with Religion in Digital Games*, edited by Heidi Campbell and Gregory P. Grieve, 109–33. Digital Game Studies. Bloomington, IN: Indiana University Press, 2014.
Spring, Dawn. "Gaming History: Computer and Video Games as Historical Scholarship." *Rethinking History* 19, no. 2 (2015): 207–21.
Taylor, Tom. "Historical Simulations and the Future of the Historical Narrative." *History and Computing* 6, no. 2 (2003).
Traxel, Oliver M. "Medieval and Pseudo-Medieval Elements in Computer Role-Playing Games: Use and Interactivity." In *Medievalism in Technology Old and New*, edited by Karl Fugelso and Carol L. Robinson, 125–42. Studies in Medievalism 16. Cambridge and Rochester, NY: D. S. Brewer, 2008.
Tyerman, Christopher. *The Debate on the Crusades*. Issues in Historiography. Manchester: Manchester University Press, 2011.
Wainwright, A. Martin. "Teaching Historical Theory through Video Games." *The History Teacher* 47, no. 4 (2014): 579–612.
Williams, D., N. Martins, M. Consalvo, and J. D. Ivory. "The Virtual Census: Representations of Gender, Race and Age in Video Games." *New Media & Society* 11, no. 5 (2009): 815–34.
Young, Helen. "Whiteness and Time: The Once, Present and Future Race." In *Medievalism on the Margins*, edited by Karl Fugelso, Vincent Ferré, and Alicia C. Montoya, 39–50. Studies in Medievalism 24. Cambridge: Boydell and Brewer, 2015.

# 1 A sacred task, no cross required

## The image of crusading in computer gaming-related non-Christian science fiction universes

*Roland Wenskus*

Popular culture is a vastly complex field which tends to be underestimated by researchers; several calls to action by historians to remedy this defect highlight the urgency of the matter.[1] Equally, the dynamics of public discourse around the theme of crusading are hard to follow and sometimes violent enough to give even the professional historian grounds to halt and self-reflect.[2] The digital age has increased the frequency of both transmission and modification of relevant material to a degree that the academic discourse is struggling to keep pace with. For instance, the present chapter hit a significant problem in its early conception when the subject matter, the examination of the image of crusading in non-Christian science fiction settings, was limited to the field of computer games.

What might sound like a trivial restriction presents the researcher with a complicated dilemma – the complexity of popular culture and the possible sub-fields. Nowadays, examining the role of a phenomenon 'in computer games' is a less than straightforward matter. The days when a video game was a hermetic thing which did not branch into any other aspect of popular culture are long gone; virtual gaming is often but one aspect of a franchise. In the case of *Star Wars*, video games were based on movies, whereas in the case of *Resident Evil*, movies were based on video games. Looking at a phenomenon like *Star Trek*, one has a set of TV series and cinematic movies influencing a nigh-uncountable number of computer games, comics, board games, novels, and so forth (without counting unlicensed content such as fan fiction), which are still all, in one way or another, part of *Star Trek*. In short, examining the previously defined role of 'crusades' in video games requires a precise working definition, so as not to lose oneself in the labyrinthine pathways of any given pop-culture franchise.

Hence, when we examine the image of crusading in video games, two criteria are set to define a thematically relevant reference, of which at least one must be fulfilled. Either the background from which a video game is derived features crusading references to a degree that they are themselves crucial to the portion of the background featured in the game (for instance, the universe of *Warhammer 40,000* and the sub-franchise-turned-video-game *Battlefleet Gothic*), or clear references must be made within a video game itself.

On topic, the notion of the crusades is a metaphor which comfortably exceeds its original definition, evolving beyond the need of a connection with Christianity.[3] This deserves a degree of scholarly attention well beyond the scope of this chapter. Hence, I have limited myself to a brief overview and analysis of this phenomenon in one of most influential aspects of popular culture – the field of science fiction – using some of the most poignant examples.

Generally, crusading references are abundant in science fiction – be it movie, TV series, or computer or tabletop game – that is, set in a hypothetical future of our own history which retains elements of our present culture. However, they are also to be found in such franchises where non-humans with no connection to Christianity employ the term, or where Earth's past history has been largely consigned to oblivion, or even in franchises set in an entirely different galaxy or universe with no possible ties to Christian religion. To examine crusading as a cultural image, be it beyond its original meaning or as an allusion to the same, it is these worlds we must turn to. The question being – if there is no connection to Christianity, what role or symbolism does the use of the word 'crusade' imply?

In the field of science fiction, one of the richest sources is the *Star Wars* franchise. With its dualism of a cosmic Force consisting of a light and dark side, the setting carries strong religious undertones. Further, the groups accessing this Force – chiefly the Jedi Knights for the Light Side and the Sith Order for the Dark Side – bear characteristics of religious organisations and even military orders. The setting is ideal for something like a holy war – or, specifically, a crusade – to occur. While only one explicit reference has so far been made in the canonical ten movies,[4] there are oblique references in all parts of the franchise, which in turn draw material from the so-called 'Legends' universe.

In April 2014, after Walt Disney acquired Lucasfilm, everything hitherto known as the 'Expanded Universe' (EU), that is, all licensed content beyond the cinematic movies and the CGI *Clone Wars* TV series by Lucasfilm Animation, was declared non-canonical and would henceforth be referred to as *Star Wars: Legends*, whereas only material released henceforth would be considered canon.[5] Making this distinction is important, considering that canonicity equates to the continued support of licensed products as well as a greater reach to a larger audience. While some of this new lore indeed referenced old canon, the bulk of crusading references are to be found in the old EU, which includes over 100 different computer games.

Separating computer game content from (former) canon outside this medium presents the researcher with the initial problem of the interaction of these media. Even with the initially pre-set criteria, drawing a line between which material to include and which to avoid is no easy task. While any *Star Wars* game can be played with little to no previous knowledge of the franchise's background, the amount of detailed and even minuscule references for the benefit of well-read fans requires elucidation by elaborating on the original material.

The number of banal medievalisms in any given part of the background is legion. Turning to the portion of the old EU set in the timespan around the canonical movies, one encounters a range of warships named 'Crusader'[6] or the like, without any further context, objects and vessels referencing in-universe undertakings called 'crusades'[7] (about which more anon), and a cavalry unit of the Royal Naboo Security Forces bizarrely named 'Royal Crusaders' created for a strategy game.[8] Of all the crusade-referencing medievalisms of the entire franchise, the latter is perhaps the least appropriate. The planet Naboo, a constitutional monarchy in the Galactic Republic, is one of the most pacifistic societies of the entire franchise.[9] For them to name an elite unit of their token armed forces – which never left the planetary system, let alone embarked on religious conquest – 'Crusaders' seems utterly out of character. If read as 'persons valiantly striving for good', it could be said to reflect the more archaic and ethically naïve streak in Naboo society. However, with these troops appearing only in a now non-canonical computer game, their cultural significance remains minor at best.

Moving on from what may be considered the 'present' of this timeline, nowhere else are 'crusading' references more in-depth than in the timeframe of the *Star Wars* chronology known as the Old Republic Era,[10] an age pre-dating the current live-action movies by several millennia. For one, crusades were a particularly popular namesake for weapons available to players in the *Star Wars: The Old Republic* massively multiplayer online roleplaying game (MMORPG).[11] Unsurprisingly, we again find a thusly named starship.[12] However, the Old Republic Era also features several warlike undertakings and groups referred to as 'crusades'[13] or 'crusaders',[14] generally featuring a religious motivation of varying degrees. The term 'crusade' is applied with little discrimination, serving to establish the settings as either valiantly noble or grimly fanatical.

One narrative arc, which has seen at least an implied re-introduction into canon, deserves our attention, the so-called Mandalorian Crusades. These serve as the primordial deed of probably the most important faction aside from Sith and Jedi, namely the Mandalorians: a human-dominated but originally multi-species warrior culture, Mandalorians and Mandalorian-influenced characters like the Republican Clone Troopers have featured prominently in a multitude of video games.[15] The *Legends* background shows them to be quite religious originally, using their crusades to forcibly spread their soteriological ideology of *Resol'Nare*.[16] It can also hardly be considered coincidence that, during their campaigns, the Mandalorians nearly wiped out a species of feline humanoids known as the Cathar.[17]

What makes these crusades so interesting is that background on Mandalorian culture is much more extensive, thus potentially offering us more insight into what might justify the name 'crusade'. This even includes a proper constructed language, or conlang, named Mando'a: first developed by British author Karen Traviss, the language is still basically considered canon, although official support has been rather muted in the last decade.[18] Yet, despite the conlang having a very active fan community, there is one very noticeable gap – namely there being no Mando'a word for the Mandalorian Crusades.[19] There is a term for the battle which ended the campaigns of a Neo-Crusader resurgence movement, namely *Ani'la Akaan* 'the Great Last Battle'[20] – but neither campaigns nor campaigners have a corresponding Mando'a word, making the choice of the name 'crusade', again, a metaphor for a religious conflict.

The question that presents itself is obvious – what justifies such a mass of references to an event the *Star Wars* universe could have no possible link to? First off, the franchise is defined by basic concepts of chivalry, with the Jedi acting as embodiments of virtue, though not infallible, similar to Arthurian protagonists, and the Sith cast in a role akin to supernaturally evil antagonists, such as the Black Knight of Chrétien de Troyes *Yvain*. It is thus no wonder that commonly accepted synonyms for 'knight' – Crusader, Paladin, Knight Errant, Gallant, Chevalier – are virtually ubiquitous in every aspect of the universe. Second, the large number of military endeavours classified as 'crusades' in the Old Republic Era is surely not a coincidence either. In the narrative of the *Star Wars* timeline, this part takes the place of an Arthurian-style medieval period, which portrays both antagonists and protagonists as much greater in power and more numerous than in the franchise's 'present', whereas the preceding timespan, known simply as 'Before the Republic', acts as a mythical dark age wherein the origins of the defining aspects of the universe are to be found. The Mandalorians, who perpetuate the myth of their crusade throughout their history within this universe, serve as the traditionalist warrior culture; a culture clinging to values that parts of the galaxy who think of themselves as more 'civilised' tend to eschew. Making the Mandalorians descendants of crusaders is an important instrument in establishing them to us Earthling consumers as the heirs to a brutal and violently expansionist warrior culture, one, while technologically advanced, we can only connect to through our own past, or rather a culturally processed modern view on it.

By comparison, the other franchise dominating the science fiction genre, *Star Trek*, is a poor resource when it comes to referencing the crusades. This can be largely attributed to its original creator, Gene Roddenberry, who took a decidedly agnostic humanist stance and ensured that any nod to religion and Christianity in particular would be kept to a minimum.[21] Thus, only a handful of explicit references to 'crusades' are to be found within the *Star Trek magnum opus*. As human culture has been largely maintained in the time leading up to the future wherein *Star Trek* is set (mostly ranging from the twenty-second to the twenty-fourth century), such allusions only interest us inasmuch as they are made by characters who do not have any reason to do so: those who lack the link to human culture that would prompt the use of such imagery. This narrows down an already small field to one major reference in the official canon of TV series and movies. It is to be found in the pilot ('The Vulcan Hello') to one of the more recent live-action TV series, *Star Trek: Discovery* (*ST: DSC*), premiered in 2017. This features an ideological resurgence of a warrior culture within a species called the Klingons, who were established early in the 1960s *Star Trek* original series as one of the chief antagonists to the Federation Starfleet (an organisation resembling a mixture of NASA and the UN Peacekeeping forces).[22] The head of this Klingon identitarian movement is one T'Kuvma, who, uncharacteristically for his kind, has an archaic religious streak: by contrast, Klingon society as previously portrayed had a decidedly atheist streak, going as far as to include the slaying of their creator gods in their myth of creation.[23]

Despite only appearing in the two pilot episodes (and in one subsequent flashback),[24] T'Kuvma's legacy has already branched out into several computer games, namely *Star Trek: Online*[25] (where his cultural impact is an important plot point in the *Age of Discovery* expansion)[26] and *Star Trek: Timelines* (where he appears as a playable character).[27] As a cultural figure, he appears as an ideologically polarising and seditious character, and it is only with reference to his character that the computer game persona can be understood, giving this crusading reference sufficient relevance despite not being directly cited in any video game. The reference itself, while comparatively oblique, does indeed help to further contextualise his character: In one of his speeches – delivered in Klingon, a conlang designed by American linguist Marc Okrand[28] – T'Kuvma proceeds to describe his struggle for Klingon rebirth as something translated as 'our crusade for self-preservation'.

Unlike Mando'a, the Klingon conlang is still officially supported and continues to develop. So, what passes as a 'crusade' in the Klingon language? According to the Klingon Language Institute, a scientific non-profit founded by psychologist Lawrence M. Schoen in 1992, dedicated to the promotion of the Klingon language and maintaining close contact with Okrand, the phrase translated as 'our crusade for self-preservation', '(ma) ghobtaHvIS', literally means '(our) ongoing fighting'.[29] So, again, this crusading reference must be understood as artistic licence rather than ideological concept. Ironically, with his pedantic adherence to religious ritual, the translation of T'Kuvma's speech better reflects his intention than the Klingon text allows for. It helps to better contextualise him within his society: He is, in every aspect – deportment, beliefs, even physical appearance – a step backwards from previous incarnations of the Klingons, which led to speculations in the fan community that he and his followers were re-awakened ancient Klingons from a sleeper ship.[30] The generally uncharacteristic hairlessness of the Klingons in Season 1 of *ST: DSC* is later revealed to be the result of ritual shearing – a traditional medieval penitential practice, which both helps to re-contextualise T'Kuvma's beliefs as archaic and explain the seeming break in continuity. His ancient ship – referred to as the *Sarcophagus* – is encrusted with reliquary pods containing the remains of fallen warriors, comes with a ceremonial funereal preparation chamber, and its bridge much more resembles the nave of a gothic cathedral than the spartan efficiency of later Klingon interior starship design. He is what might come closest to a medievalism-style religious fanatic in the context of Klingon culture.

The computer game best reflecting this can be said to be *Star Trek: Timelines*, designed mostly for mobile devices and browser play mode.[31] Its gameplay is comparatively simple, resembling a 1990s roleplaying game, with playable characters represented through a simple system of proficiency stats and character keywords. As a playable character, T'Kuvma features the keywords *Klingon, Brutal, Hero, Cultural Figure,* and *Spiritual.* The 'Klingon' aside, these characteristics match up exactly with the popular imagination of a crusader, and even with the perception of crusaders as focal points of cultural identity, similar to the appropriation of such medievalism by the political far-right.

This is very much in keeping with the popular perception of the character itself; fans and commentators were quick to identify him and his followers as metaphors for current political far-right movements in the USA.[32] This association is hardly a coincidence. In any given period, *Star Trek* was anything but apolitical, which gives a clear indication as to the timing of T'Kuvma's speech: when *Star Trek: The Original Series* (*ST: TOS*) was a veiled commentary on the Cold War and its ramifications, and *Star Trek: Enterprise* (*ST: ENT*) made strong references towards the 9/11 attacks and terrorism in general, *Discovery* concerned itself with the recent rise in violent racial supremacism.[33] Given the popularity of the crusading medievalism among identitarian and related alt-right groups, the usage of the medievalism is twofold: for one, there is the 'direct medievalism' of characterising T'Kuvma as the equivalent to a pop-culture crusader. On a second level, T'Kuvma's referencing of identitarian-typical usage of medievalism can be said to constitute a reflection on this type of medievalism itself.[34] Moreover, the futuristic setting allows for an almost impossible combination of two variations of extremist ideology: by discrediting the Federation as a place where the Klingons would be, as T'Kuvma put it, dragged 'into the muck where humans, Vulcans, Tellarites, and filthy Andorians mix', his words echo the racially charged polemic of older right-wing extremists, while his acceptance of Voq, a Klingon albino (whose skin colour causes them to be social outcasts), into his house mirrors the more modern, culture-focused extremism espoused by terrorists like Anders Breivik.[35] The character can thus be said to be a double metaphor: the fanatic of past times and the fanatic of the present.

The science fiction universe with undoubtedly the most plot-carrying references to crusades, however, has to be the universe of *Warhammer 40,000* (*Wh40k*). As it is comparatively less well known, I shall give a brief summary of its premise: it revolves around the galaxy-spanning human Imperium in the year 40,000 AD. Said Imperium, now a fascistic theocracy, started in the year 30,000 AD, when a semi-mythical *Übermensch* known solely as the Emperor re-united the warring nations of Earth following a millennia-long dark age. Aided by legions of regular human soldiers and genetically modified post-human warriors referred to as 'Space Marines', he re-established contact with the scattered human colonies throughout the galaxy, turning the Milky Way into a human-dominated empire under constant threat from aliens and much more esoteric threats. These threats, largely revolving around evil incorporeal creatures known as the Chaos Gods and their minions, both mortal and other, prompted the Emperor to establish a doctrine of state atheism known as *The Creed of the Imperial Truth*, to prevent nourishing these creatures by allowing superstition to grow into actual cults. Yet paradoxically, this fiercely anti-religious ruler would name the military campaign designed to unite the galaxy under humanity's rule as 'The Great Crusade', a bewildering contradiction addressed in the short story 'The Last Church', wherein the Emperor's troops set out to obliterate the last remaining house of worship, to face its guardian priest named Uriah – who, after a long sermon by the Emperor about why religion must be done away with, is outraged when he learns that the proposed campaign shall be named 'Great Crusade':

'Didn't you just tell me of the bloody slaughters perpetrated by crusaders?' said Uriah. 'Doesn't that make you no better than the holy men you were telling me about?'
'The difference is I know I am right,' said the Emperor.
'Spoken like a true autocrat.'
The Emperor shook his head. 'You misunderstand, Uriah. I have seen the narrow survival path that is all that stands between humanity and extinction, and this is the way it must begin.'
Uriah looked back at the church, the gleeful flames reaching high into the darkness.
'It is a dangerous road you travel,' said Uriah. 'To deny humanity a thing will only make them crave it all the more. And if you succeed in this grand vision of yours? What then? Beware that your subjects do not begin to see you as a god.'[36]

Needless to say, Uriah's words prove to be prophetic and the Emperor fails in a grand way: betrayed and grievously wounded by his most trusted warlord Horus,[37] he falls into a deathless coma, while, for the next ten millennia, the Imperium of Humankind deteriorates into a backward theocracy, placing the Emperor into the centre of the Imperial Cult. In its zeal, the Imperium launches an uncounted number of large-scale campaigns named 'crusades', while renegades sworn to the Chaos Gods launch their own campaigns called 'Black Crusades', as a twisted parody of their Imperial counterpart. The most recent background expansion saw Roboute Guilliman, gene-father (Primarch) of the Space Marine legion (later chapter) known as the Ultramarines and one of the Emperor's most trusted lieutenants awakening from an Arthurian-style state of near-death. Lamenting the state of spiritual narrow-mindedness mankind has entered, he immediately calls for a great campaign to reassert Imperial authority, which he, in the contradictory tradition of the Emperor, names the Indomitus Crusade.[38]

Also, the naming continuity shown in *Warhammer 40,000* is clearly designed to reflect the transition from Late Antiquity to the Middle Ages. For example, Space Marines, previously organised in legions, are now being re-formed into chapters, some of which take on a nomadic lifestyle as so-called 'crusading chapters'. The present of *Wh40k* is, with an Inquisition culling inner enemies, intimidating gothic architecture brooding over the downtrodden citizenry, and opponents best described as elves, orcs, and demons in space, by design supposed to be a fantasised medieval universe transposed into the far future – a medieval theme underlined by the image of the crusade.

One Space Marine chapter which deserves special attention is the Black Templars, one of the 'crusading chapters' founded shortly after the Emperor's fall: their heraldry already largely consists of a jumble of elements loaned from the imagery of the Knights Templar, the Knights Hospitaller, and the Teutonic Order,[39] while their galaxy-spanning network of self-sufficient chapter houses strongly resembles the commandries of the aforementioned three confraternities.[40] Even their individual titles largely consist of chivalric and monastic medievalisms, with the ranks referred to as 'Captain' in most other chapters called 'Marshal' and the rank of 'Lieutenant' being supplanted by 'Castellan', 'Veterans' are referred to as 'Sword Brethren', the rank-and-file named 'Initiates', and new recruits to the order called 'Neophytes', who also serve in a squire-like capacity to senior brothers.[41]

The Black Templars stand out insofar as the medieval theme has been taken to an extreme which even goes beyond the eventual evolution of Space Marines to interstellar military orders. In the original 1987 first edition of *Wh40k*, the military order theme was already apparent, but the depiction also still bore a strong semblance to cinematic depictions of the United States Marine Corps, complete with stereotypical characters (Chaplain, Medic, Tech, Captain, Military Police).[42] The further the edition progressed, the more the imagery was shifted towards military orders: Military Police were scrapped, while Medics were re-named to Apothecaries, crude slogans like 'KIL KIL KIL' daubed on the armour were replaced with litanies in 'High Gothic' (a ceremonial language resembling butchered Latin),[43] and the design of the equipment increasingly reflected its status as venerated technological relics rather than the previous optics of factory-fresh high-tech gear.[44] When the background to the Black Templars was further fleshed out, this chivalric-monastic undertone was taken to further extremes, showing the brothers of the chapter to wear tabards (and Sword Brethren even a chlamys), scribbling devotional litanies onto random pieces of armour, and, eventually, being described as worshipping the Emperor as a God (which, while expected of non-modified humans – and brutally enforced in case of non-compliance – is said to be an exception among the post-human Space Marines).[45] In a galaxy roamed by superhuman knightly orders, the Black Templars were shown to be an extreme of extremes in every sense.

While no Black Templar has been featured as a main character in the continuously growing range of licensed *Warhammer 40,000* computer games so far, they do make a notable appearance in the 2011 game *Space Marine*: a retinue of this chapter is shown to accompany the representative of the Imperial Inquisition sent to place the protagonist of the game into custody.[46]

Their appearance at that instance is no coincidence either: in their role as futuristic crusaders, they are the perfect companions to a representative of the Inquisition, the zealots to act as the muscle for the merciless fanatic. This impression is further intensified by the nature of the protagonist, who is borne away to an uncertain fate: Captain Titus of the Ultramarines chapter serves as the counterpoint to the brooding medievalism-rich atmosphere of the game. The Ultramarines, as the gene-sons of Roboute Guilliman, are a notable contrast to the Black Templars as they are portrayed to be warrior-philosophers with a strong humanist streak and a tendency to employ the imagery of Roman and Greek Antiquity rather than that of the European Middle Ages.[47] Their *Weltanschauung*, as heirs to one of the first Space Marine Legions, chiefly reflects the scholarly secularist traditions of the Imperium prior to Horus' betrayal, while the Black Templars, founded from the more radical elements of the Imperial Fists Legion following the schism, are an image of what became of the Imperium following this war of brothers.[48] With popular historicisms tending to portray classical Antiquity as an age of proto-Enlightenment then suffering a crushing setback through the allegedly barbaric Middle Ages, the scene encapsulates the essence of the crusading medievalism – the implacable crusaders crushing the reflected humanism of an age past.

Turning to the Lovecraftian cults followed by the Space Marines sworn to Horus and the Chaos Gods, the crusading imagery remains very present despite their renunciation of all ties with the Imperium and its doctrines. Their 'Black Crusades' featured in the *Battlefleet Gothic* video game franchise – a computer game adaptation of Games Workshop's discontinued fleet-based strategy tabletop game set in the *Warhammer 40,000* universe – are shown as one of the major threats to the Imperium, with the Chaos worshippers' most recent advances culminating in the catastrophic events which provide the current setting for *Wh40k*.

It is debatable to what extent these 'Black Crusades' can be considered medievalisms or rather are to be understood as explicit references to Imperial Crusades, which would make the medievalism rather secondary. The sheer maelstrom of destruction unleashed opens up either interpretation, particularly with the obvious religious themes of war as a sacred act (destruction wrought to satisfy the Chaos Gods, albeit often with deeply personal motives)[49] and even the historically crusade-specific theme of casting down false idols (with 'Death to the False Emperor'[50] being a particularly popular rallying cry among the Chaos-worshipping Space Marines).

Looking back on the field of science fiction, the crusade as a universal term beyond a simple medievalism is ubiquitous. Ranging from passing and debatably appropriate uses to elaborately thought-out and applied terminology, the computer games of the genre offer the researcher a near-limitless reservoir of investigative possibilities.

To conclude, three themes have become apparent in the search for the specific use of crusading imagery:

1. 'This is supposed to be medieval'
2. 'A noble cause/a sacred task'
3. 'A fanatic's (sometimes vain) pursuit'

Moreover, the signifier is used in such a manner which suggests the authors were in no doubt that of these rather divergent meanings, the target audience would understand the intended one. However random and banal it may sound, there is no doubt that the 'Royal Naboo Crusaders' would never be understood as brutal, expansionist fanatics. Likewise, no one would think of the Chaos Space Marines' 'Black Crusades' as idealistic endeavours designed to further noble causes. The de-Christianised use of 'crusade' is in almost all cases specific enough to elicit the intended association without further explanation. In any given case, the representation of the crusading metaphors still strongly rely upon shared perceptions of the historical crusades, which in turn are strong enough to survive the dissociation from the immediate Christian context.

These examples show us that 'crusading', as a cultural concept, has evolved beyond the need of its original constitutive factors, provided it can still rely on such abstract conceptions. These conceptions, as this work hopes to show, are an elaborate mixture of medievalisms, reflections upon medievalisms, and attempts at reflecting on established concepts of history, as far as that distinction can be drawn. They rely on a remarkably complex collective understanding of the term 'crusade', one which is likely to continue to inspire and reinforce a rich, sometimes problematic, but nonetheless significant cultural heritage – irrespective of any direct association with established Earth religious concepts. Hence, it can be said with some conviction that, should the idea of Christianity ever become naught but a distant memory, people will still be 'crusading' merrily on.

## Notes

1 See, for instance, Kristin Skottki, "The Dead, the Revived and the Recreated Pasts: 'Structural Amnesia' in Representations of Crusade History," in *Perceptions of the Crusades from the Nineteenth to the Twenty-First Century: Engaging the Crusades, Volume One*, ed. Mike Horswell and Jonathan Phillips (Abingdon: Routledge, 2018), 79–106.
2 Susanna A. Throop, "Engaging the Crusades in Context: Reflections on the Ethics of Historical Work," in *The Crusades in the Modern World: Engaging the*

*Crusades, Volume Two*, ed. Mike Horswell and Akil N. Awan (Abingdon: Routledge, 2020), 129–45.

3   The use of the term (particularly in political debate) has consequently been criticised; see Matthew Gabriele, "Debating the 'Crusade' in Contemporary America," *The Mediaeval Journal* 6, no. 1 (2016): 73–92.

4   "He feared you might follow old Obi-Wan on some damn fool idealistic crusade like your father did." – Obi-Wan Kenobi to Luke Skywalker, in reference to Luke's uncle, Owen Lars. *Star Wars: Episode IV – A New Hope* (1977).

5   *StarWars.com*, "The Legendary Star Wars Expanded Universe Turns a New Page," April 25, 2014, www.starwars.com/news/the-legendary-star-wars-expanded-universe-turns-a-new-page, accessed March 1, 2018.

6   Such as the Imperial Victory-class Star Destroyer "Crusader" appearing in the video game *Star Wars: Empire at War* (LucasArts, 2006).

7   Namely the Crusader-class corvette, in service with both the Galactic Empire and the Mandalorians first appearing in the *Forces of Corruption* expansion to the video game *Star Wars*, or the Mandalorian Crusader Templar sword from the defunct Star Wars MMORPG, *Star Wars Galaxies: An Empire Divided* (LucasArts, 2003–11).

8   Appearing in the computer strategy game *Star Wars: Galactic Battlegrounds* (LucasArts, 2001).

9   For a brief introduction, see *StarWars.com*, "Databank: Naboo," www.starwars.com/databank/naboo, accessed June 24, 2018.

10  From 25,053 BBY (the founding of the Galactic Republic, BBY meaning "Before the Battle of Yavin," i.e. the events surrounding the plot of the first *Star Wars* movie), until 1000 BBY (the end of the New Sith Wars and the beginning of the Rise of the Empire Era until 0 BBY).

11  Ten of these are blaster cannons (the C-106 Night Hunter Crusader, Ion-X-Crusader, Ion-XX Crusader, M-315 Laser Crusader, Nova Crusader, R-20 Watchman Crusader, Rancor Crusader and the not identical A-12 Rancor Crusader, U-113 Sentry Crusader, and the Z-303 Rotary Crusader) and one sonic cannon (the N-416 Heavy Sonic Crusader). See *Star Wars: The Old Republic* (LucasArts, 2011).

12  The attack cruiser Justice Crusader in service to the Jedi Order. First appearing in: Drew Karpyshyn, *Darth Bane: Rule of Two* (New York, NY: Del Rey/Random House Publishing, 2007).

13  Notably the Pius Dea Crusades, a series of campaigns by a militaristic subfaction of religious fanatics known as the *Pius Dea*, monotheistic humanocentric autocrats who had usurped the chancellorship of the Republic (see Jason Fry and Paul R. Urquhart, *Star Wars: The Essential Guide to Warfare* (New York, NY: Del Rey/Random House Publishing, 2012), 25–28), and the Krath Holy Crusade engineered by a Sith-emulating cult (first appearing in Tom Veitch et al., *Star Wars: Tales of the Jedi – The Freedon Nadd Uprising* (Milwaukie, OR: Dark Horse Comics, 1994).

14  Particularly the Spumani Crusaders, a religious cult operating during the New Sith Wars (2000–1000 BBY, group mentioned in *StarWars.com*, "Essential Atlas Extra: The Knight Errant Gazetter," November 12, 2012, www.starwars.com/news/essential-atlas-extra-the-knight-errant-gazetter, accessed June 24, 2018), and the renegade Jedi followers of Revan, known both as "Revanchists" and "Jedi Crusaders" (first mentioned in *Star Wars: Knights of the Old Republic* (LucasArts, 2003).

15 Such as *Star Wars: Bounty Hunter* (LucasArts, 2002); *Star Wars: Battlefront II* (LucasArts, 2005); or *Star Wars: Republic Commando* (LucasArts, 2005).
16 Mando'a for "Six Actions." See Karen Traviss, "The Mandalorians: People and Culture," *Star Wars Insider* 86 (2006): 20.
17 See Fry and Urquhart, *Star Wars: The Essential Guide to Warfare*, 38–39.
18 Songs in Mando'a featured prominently in the first-person shooter *Star Wars: Republic Commando*.
19 The fan community at *mandoa.org* is always happy to answer questions for those interested.
20 See Fry and Urquhart, *Star Wars: The Essential Guide to Warfare*, 40–41.
21 See Anne McKenzie Pearson, "From Thwarted Gods to Reclaimed Mystery? An Overview of the Depiction of Religion in Star Trek," in *Star Trek and Sacred Ground: Explorations of Star Trek, Religion, and American Culture*, ed. Jennifer E. Porter and Darcee L. McLaren (Albany, NY: State University of New York Press, 1999), 13–32, particularly 14–17.
22 With regard to the ill-defined legal status of Starfleet, see Christian Wagnsonner and Stefan Gugerel, eds., *Star Trek für Auslandseinsätze? Konfliktstrategien und Lösungsansätze für reale Probleme in Science fiction* (Vienna: Institut für Religion und Frieden, 2011).
23 See "You are Cordially Invited," *Star Trek: Deep Space Nine* season 6 episode 7 (Paramount Domestic Television, 1997), as they were originally intended to be a metaphorical depiction of the Soviet Union (see Marty P. Taylor, ed., *Star Trek: Adventures in Time and Space* (New York, NY: Pocket Books, 1999), 292.).
24 "The Vulcan Hello," "Battle at the Binary Stars" and "The Wolf Inside," *Star Trek: Discovery* Season 1 Episodes 1, 2 and 11 (CBS Home Entertainment, 2017/18).
25 *Star Trek: Online* (Cryptic Studios/Atari Interactive, 2010).
26 "Age of Discovery," *Star Trek: Online* (Cryptic Studios/Perfect World, 2018).
27 *Star Trek: Timelines* (Disruptor Beam, 2016).
28 First fully developed for *Star Trek III: The Search for Spock* (Paramount Pictures, 1984). Further developed in Marc Okrand, *The Klingon Dictionary* (New York, NY: Pocket Books, 1992); Marc Okrand, *Klingon for the Galactic Traveler* (New York, NY: Pocket Books, 1997).
29 The full exchange to be found at *kli.org*, www.kli.org/question/what-is-the-klingon-word-for-crusade/#, accessed August 15, 2019.
30 Similar to the Klingon sleeper ship IKS T'Ong in: "The Emissary," *Star Trek: The Next Generation*, Season 2 Episode 20 (Paramount Domestic Television, 1989). See Ryan Britt, "There's a Klingon Sarcophagus Ship in 'Star Trek: Discovery'," *inverse.com*, July 21, 2017, www.inverse.com/article/34502-klingon-sarcophagus-ship-star-trek-discovery-comiccon-mek-leth, accessed August 15, 2019.
31 Further information at the game's official web site: *disruptorbeam.com*, www.disruptorbeam.com/games/star-trek-timelines, accessed August 15, 2019.
32 Kaleigh Rogers, "'Star Trek: Discovery' Effortlessly Demonstrates Why TV Needs More Diversity," *Vice.com*, September 25, 2017, www.vice.com/en_us/article/kz73wn/star-trek-discovery-effortlessly-demonstrates-why-tv-needs-more-diversity, accessed August 18, 2019. For a negative (while still positive towards the show) reaction on this perspective, see Matt Gurney, "Attention, Star Trek Culture Warriors: Stand Down from Battle Stations," *Quillette.com*,

January 29, 2019, https://quillette.com/2019/01/29/attention-star-trek-culture-warriors-stand-down-from-battle-stations/, accessed August 18, 2019.
33 For a general introduction with a specific focus on *ST: TOS* see George A. Gonzalez, *The Politics of Star Trek: Justice, War, and the Future* (New York, NY: Palgrave Macmillan, 2015); for *ST: ENT* see Lincoln Geraghty, *American Science Fiction Film and Television* (Oxford and New York, NY: Berg Publishers, 2009), 104; Amy M. Damico, "Television," in *September 11 in Popular Culture: A guide*, ed. Sara E Quay and Amy M. Damico (Santa Barbara, CA: Greenwood, 2010), 142. For *ST: DSC* see George A. Gonzalez, *Justice and Popular Culture: Star Trek as Philosophical Text* (London: Lexington Books, 2019), 29–31.
34 For a comprehensive study of the appropriation in particular of the crusading theme within various far-right movements see Andrew B. R. Elliott, *Medievalism, Politics, and Mass Media: Appropriating the Middle Ages in the Twenty-First Century* (Cambridge: D. S. Brewer, 2017).
35 On the evolution of right-wing extremism in this context see Daniel Wollenberg, "The New Knighthood: Terrorism and the Medieval," *Postmedieval* 5 (2014): 29–30.
36 Dan Abnett, "The Last Church," in *Tales of Heresy*, ed. Nick Kyme and Lindsey Priestley (Nottingham: Black Library, 2009), 371–73.
37 The events of this period commonly called the "Horus Heresy" have been featured in several video games, most notably *Horus Heresy: Drop Assault* (Nottingham: Black Library, Complex Games, 2015), *Talisman: The Horus Heresy* (Nottingham: Black Library, Nomad Games, 2016), *The Horus Heresy: Battle of Tallarn* (Nottingham: Black Library, HexWar Games, 2017), and *The Horus Heresy: Legions* (Nottingham: Black Library, Everguild, 2019).
38 "Why do I live? What do you want from me? I put everything into our dream, and look what they've done! An empire of fear, hate and ignorance – better we had all burned in the fires of Horus' ambition than live to see this." Gav Thorpe, *Rise of the Primarch* (Nottingham: Games Workshop, 2017), 40.
39 Their complete heraldry was first showcased in Graham McNeill, *Codex: Black Templars* (Nottingham: Games Workshop, 2005), 50. While the heraldry of the rank-and-file battle-brothers obviously chiefly draws from the Teutonic Order (although in the post-medieval form rather than the more common Latin cross of the 13th century; see Hartmut Boockmann, *Der Deutsche Orden – Zwölf Kapitel aus seiner Geschichte* (Munich: Beck, 1981), 303.), the inverted form worn by chaplains evokes the habit worn by the Knights of St. John: see Jonathan Riley-Smith, *The Knights of St. John in Jerusalem and Cyprus c. 1050–1310* (London: Palgrave Macmillan, 1967), 323. While the red cross on black ground worn by the formation of veterans known as Sword Brethren (again a nod to yet another historic knightly order: see Friedrich Benninghoven, *Der Orden der Schwertbrüder* (Cologne: Böhlau, 1965)) resembles the heraldry of the sergeants of the Knights Templar: see Judith Mary Upton-Ward, ed., *The Rule of the Templars* (Woodbridge: Boydell & Brewer, 1997), 54.
40 Gav Thorpe, "Righteous Zeal – The Black Templars Space Marine Chapter," *Index Astartes* 2 (2003): 45; also McNeill, *Codex: Black Templars*, 8. For a comprehensive overview of the respective continental administrative structures of the Military Orders see Karl Borchardt, "The Military-Religious Orders in the Crusader West," in *The Crusader World*, ed. Adrian Boas (London and New York, NY: Routledge, 2016), 111–27.

41  See McNeill, *Codex: Black Templars*, 12–15.
42  See Rick Priestley et al., *Warhammer 40.000 – Rogue Trader* (Nottingham: Games Workshop, 1987), 154–56, 168–69.
43  *Chaos Gate* (Nottingham: Random Games/Strategic Simulations, 1998) even featured a mixture of historical Latin texts (the *Dies irae/Regis regum rectissimi* by St. Columba the Elder) and home-made lyrics, which still come closer to actual Latin that the "High Gothic" from the average Games Workshop publication. For further information on "High Gothic" also see Otta Wenskus, "X-treme Latin, Schnodder-Synchro und Verwandtes," in *Pontes V: Übersetzung als Vermittlerin antiker Literatur*, ed. Wolfgang Kofler, Florian Schaffenrath and Karlheinz Töchterle (Innsbruck: Studien Verlag, 2009), 352–64.
44  The use of so-called "personal litanies" harkens back to the first background article addressing the Black Templars: see Thorpe, "Righteous Zeal – The Black Templars Space Marine Chapter," 45. A most notable example of technology being viewed as sacred relics rather than mere machines of war are the war walkers generally referred to as Dreadnoughts. For an in-game perspective on their status, see Graham McNeill, Pete Haines, and Andy Chambers, "Warriors of Old – Space Marine Dreadnoughts," *Index Astartes* 1 (2002): 52–57.
45  Robin Cruddace, *Codex: Space Marines* (Nottingham: Games Workshop, 2012), 51 was the first to explicitly state this belief, which has been re-affirmed in every edition since, though first hints at this ideology could already be found in Ben Counter, "Words of Blood," in *Words of Blood*, ed. Marc Gascoigne and Christian Dunn (Nottingham: Black Library, 2002), 23.
46  *Warhammer 40.000: Space Marine* (Relic Entertainment/THQ, 2011).
47  The Ultramarines' ancestral realm of "Ultramar" was, in all likelihood, chosen to serve as a near-homonym to the chapter name, rather than as an explicit reference to the "Outremer" of the Crusader States. Its condition, thanks to the guidance of its superhuman overlords, is described as a marked contrast to the often dystopian industrial wastelands of other Imperial worlds; see Matthew Ward, *Codex: Space Marines* (Nottingham: Games Workshop, 2008), 14–16. A particularly relevant overview of Ultramarines imagery can be found ibid., 20–23.
48  For a short overview of Ultramarines tenets, see Graham McNeill, "Warriors of Ultramar – The Ultramarines Space Marines Chapter," *Index Astartes* 3 (2003): 28–29; for the secularism inherent to most Space Marine Chapters see Anthony Reynolds, "For the Emperor – Space Marine Chaplains," *Index Astartes* 2 (2003): 57–59.
49  For an overview of the Thirteen Black Crusades see Robin Cruddace, *Codex: Black Legion* (Nottingham: Games Workshop, 2013), 16–27.
50  A phrase – from a background perspective – first coined by Captain Jago "Sevatar" Sevatarion of the Night Lords Traitor Legion in the context of the first major betrayal against the Imperium (see Aaron Dembski-Bowden, *The Horus Heresy – The First Heretic* (Nottingham: Black Library, 2010), 413–22.).

## Bibliography

Abnett, Dan. "The Last Church." In *Tales of Heresy*, edited by Nick Kyme and Lindsey Priestley, 323–74. Nottingham: Black Library, 2009.
Benninghoven, Friedrich. *Der Orden der Schwertbrüder*. Cologne: Böhlau, 1965.

Boockmann, Hartmut. *Der Deutsche Orden – Zwölf Kapitel aus seiner Geschichte*. Munich: Beck, 1981.

Borchardt, Karl. "The Military-Religious Orders in the Crusader West." In *The Crusader World*, edited by Adrian Boas, 111–27. London and New York, NY: Routledge, 2016.

Britt, Ryan. "There's a Klingon Sarcophagus Ship in 'Star Trek: Discovery'." *inverse.com*, July 21, 2017, www.inverse.com/article/34502-klingon-sarcophagus-ship-star-trek-discovery-comiccon-mek-leth. Accessed August 15, 2019.

*Codex: Space Marines*. Nottingham: Games Workshop, 2013.

Counter, Ben. "Words of Blood." In *Words of Blood*, edited by Marc Gascoigne and Christian Dunn, 7–32. Nottingham: Black Library, 2002.

Cruddace, Robin. *Codex: Black Legion*. Nottingham: Games Workshop, 2013.

Damico, Amy M. "Television." In *September 11 in Popular Culture: A Guide*, edited by Sara E. Quay and Amy M. Damico, 131–72. Santa Barbara, CA: Greenwood, 2010.

Dembski-Bowden, Aaron. *The Horus Heresy – The First Heretic*. Nottingham: Black Library, 2010.

*disruptorbeam.com*. www.disruptorbeam.com/games/star-trek-timelines. Accessed August 1, 2019.

Elliott, Andrew B. R. *Medievalism, Politics, and Mass Media: Appropriating the Middle Ages in the Twenty-First Century*. Cambridge: D. S. Brewer, 2017.

Fry, Jason, and Paul R. Urquhart. *Star Wars: The Essential Guide to Warfare*. New York, NY: Del Rey/Random House Publishing, 2012.

Gabriele, Matthew. "Debating the 'Crusade' in Contemporary America." *The Mediaeval Journal* 6, no. 1 (2016): 73–92.

Geraghty, Lincoln. *American Science Fiction Film and Television*. Oxford and New York, NY: Berg Publishers, 2009.

Gonzalez, George A. *Justice and Popular Culture: Star Trek as Philosophical Text*. London: Lexington Books, 2019.

———. *The Politics of Star Trek: Justice, War, and the Future*. New York, NY: Palgrave Macmillan, 2015.

Gurney, Matt. "Attention, Star Trek Culture Warriors: Stand Down from Battle Stations." *Quillette.com*, January 29, 2019. https://quillette.com/2019/01/29/attention-star-trek-culture-warriors-stand-down-from-battle-stations/. Accessed August 18, 2019.

Karpyshyn, Drew. *Darth Bane: Rule of Two*. New York, NY: Del Rey/Random House Publishing, 2007.

McKenzie Pearson, Ann. "From Thwarted Gods to Reclaimed Mystery? An Overview of the Depiction of Religion in Star Trek." In *Star Trek and Sacred Ground: Explorations of Star Trek, Religion, and American Culture*, edited by Jennifer E. Porter and Darcee L. McLaren, 13–32. Albany, NY: State University of New York Press, 1999.

McNeill, Graham. *Codex: Black Templars*. Nottingham: Games Workshop, 2005.

———. "Warriors of Ultramar – The Ultramarines Space Marines Chapter." *Index Astartes* 3 (2003): 22–29.

McNeill, Graham, Pete Haines, and Andy Chambers. "Warriors of Old – Space Marine Dreadnoughts." *Index Astartes* 1 (2002): 52–57.

Okrand, Marc. *Klingon for the Galactic Traveler*. New York, NY: Pocket Books, 1997.

———. *The Klingon Dictionary*. New York, NY: Pocket Books, 1992.

Priestley, Rick et al. *Warhammer 40.000 – Rogue Trader*. Nottingham: Games Workshop, 1987.

Reynolds, Anthony. "For the Emperor – Space Marine Chaplains." *Index Astartes* 2 (2003): 56–59.

Riley-Smith, Jonathan. *The Knights of St. John in Jerusalem and Cyprus c. 1050–1310*. London: Palgrave Macmillan, 1967.

Rogers, Kaleigh. " 'Star Trek: Discovery' Effortlessly Demonstrates Why TV Needs More Diversity." *Vice.com*, September 25, 2017. www.vice.com/en_us/article/kz73wn/star-trek-discovery-effortlessly-demonstrates-why-tv-needs-more-diversity. Accessed August 18, 2019.

Skottki, Kristin. "The Dead, the Revived and the Recreated Pasts: 'Structural Amnesia' in Representations of Crusade History." In *Perceptions of the Crusades from the Nineteenth to the Twenty-First Century: Engaging the Crusades, Volume One*, edited by Mike Horswell and Jonathan Phillips, 79–106. Abingdon: Routledge, 2018.

*StarWars.com*. "Databank: Naboo." www.starwars.com/databank/naboo. Accessed June 24, 2018.

———. "Essential Atlas Extra: The Knight Errant Gazetter," November 12, 2012. www.starwars.com/news/essential-atlas-extra-the-knight-errant-gazetter. Accessed June 24, 2018.

———. "The Legendary Star Wars Expanded Universe Turns a New Page," April 25, 2014. www.starwars.com/news/the-legendary-star-wars-expanded-universe-turns-a-new-page. Accessed March 1, 2018.

Taylor, Marty P., ed. *Star Trek: Adventures in Time and Space*. New York, NY: Pocket Books, 1999.

Thorpe, Gav. "Righteous Zeal – The Black Templars Space Marine Chapter." *Index Astartes* 2 (2013): 44–55.

———. *Rise of the Primarch*. Nottingham: Games Workshop, 2017.

Throop, Susanna A. "Engaging the Crusades in Context: Reflections on the Ethics of Historical Work." In *The Crusades in the Modern World: Engaging the Crusades, Volume Two*, edited by Mike Horswell and Akil N. Awan, 129–45. Abingdon: Routledge, 2020.

Traviss, Karen. "The Mandalorians: People and Culture." *Star Wars Insider* 86 (2006): 18–26.

Upton-Ward, Judith Mary, ed. *The Rule of the Templars*. Woodbridge: Boydell & Brewer, 1997.

Veitch, Tom et al. *Star Wars: Tales of the Jedi – The Freedon Nadd Uprising*, 2 vols. Milwaukie, OR: Dark Horse Comics, 1994.

Wagnsonner, Christian, and Gugerel Stefan, eds. *Star Trek für Auslandseinsätze? Konfliktstrategien und Lösungsansätze für reale Probleme in Science fiction*. Vienna: Institut für Religion und Frieden, 2011.

Ward, Matthew. *Codex: Space Marines*. Nottingham: Games Workshop, 2008.
Wenskus, Otta. "X-treme Latin, Schnodder-Synchro und Verwandtes." In *Pontes V: Übersetzung als Vermittlerin antiker Literatur*, edited by Wolfgang Kofler, Florian Schaffenrath, and Karlheinz Töchterle, 352–64. Innsbruck: Studien Verlag, 2009.
"What is the Klingon Word for Crusade?" *kli.org*. www.kli.org/question/what-is-the-klingon-word-for-crusade/#. Accessed August 15, 2019.
Wollenberg, Daniel. "The New Knighthood: Terrorism and the Medieval." *Postmedieval* 5 (2014): 21–33.

## 2 'I'm not responsible for the man you are!'
### Crusading and masculinities in *Dante's Inferno*[1]

*Katherine J. Lewis*

Since its earliest iteration in the late eleventh century crusading has been perceived as a quintessentially masculine undertaking. Consequently, in both medieval and modern narratives the crusades function as a crucible in which manhood is tested; its quality thereby either confirmed or exposed as inadequate.[2] When examining such depictions of crusading masculinities it is essential to consider the socio-cultural contexts in which they are produced and the ideological purposes which they serve. As Andrew B. R. Elliott and Mike Horswell state, we must ask: '*who* is remembering the crusades and *why*?'[3] With these issues in mind, the ensuing discussion elucidates the gendered implications of the reimagining of Dante as a veteran of the Third Crusade (1189–1192) in *Dante's Inferno*. The real Dante (d. 1321) was not a crusader and lived a century after the Third Crusade, but *Dante's Inferno* was never intended to be a faithful adaptation of the poem. Jonathan Knight, co-writer and co-producer, emphasised that the game was loosely inspired by Dante's *Inferno*, locating it as part of a centuries-old tradition of adapting and reworking the poem in different media and for different audiences.[4] Indeed, the transformation of Dante from poet to crusader is its most striking and revealing departure from the source. In so doing the game enacts a number of well-established modern preconceptions about crusading. *Dante's Inferno* rewards analysis for the creative ways in which crusading is used to provide context for Dante's character, as a test of his manhood, and to explore issues of personal morality and culpability.

*Dante's Inferno* is a hack-and-slash action adventure game developed by Visceral Arts (a subsidiary of EA). It is based on Dante Aligheri's *Inferno*, the first Canto of his early fourteenth-century *Divina Commedia*, and was released in 2010.[5] The player controls Dante on his journey through Hell. Dante fights demons with a melee weapon (Death's scythe) and a ranged weapon (the Holy Cross), and has the power to either punish or absolve both mobs and the famous souls whom he encounters. Puzzle solving and a gauntlet of combat challenges also feature. Ten years on the game still looks good, with well-conceived visuals giving a distinctive appearance to each level and its demon-mobs, which, combined with atmospheric music, render it impressive and unsettling.[6] Indeed, the game's appearance garnered a good deal of praise from reviewers and it was fairly well-received on release, although some felt that it ran out of creative steam, becoming repetitive towards the end.[7] The main criticism from both reviewers and players focused on perceptions that *Dante's Inferno* was, essentially, an inferior *God of War* (2005–2018) rip-off. Although the extent of Knight's appreciation for the poem and his knowledge of the history of its adaptation was often acknowledged.[8] The game's original website included background information about Dante, *Inferno*, and the broader historical context, intended to encourage players to find out more about the source material.[9] Furthermore, as part of the game's publicity an edition of Longfellow's translation of *Inferno* was published, with the same cover as the game, including an introduction by Knight as well as illustrations from the game.[10] Knight claimed that he had been contacted by teachers who said that the game had actually stimulated students' interest in the poem.[11] Indeed, Brandon K. Essary has recently discussed his positive experiences of using *Dante's Inferno* to teach Dante's poem to undergraduates.[12] Additionally, many players clearly enjoyed, and still enjoy, the game, as witness the many positive assessments left underneath a full walkthrough posted on YouTube in July 2019.[13]

There has been some excellent scholarly analysis of Dante's masculinity in relation to the game's use of the original poem and its appropriation of medieval motifs more generally. For example, Oliver Chadwick discusses the game's reworking of medieval courtly masculinities, arguing that this demonstrates 'how the *medieval* past is implicated in the construction and definition of *contemporary* masculinities'.[14] He contends that the experience of playing Dante buttresses a conventional form of hegemonic masculinity predicated on prowess, aggression, and physical dominance of others which is rendered specifically medieval by the courtly narrative frame.[15] By contrast Denise A. Ayo argues that far from presenting a simplistic, laudatory depiction of hypermasculinity, the game's unfolding narrative 'oscillates between supporting and dismantling stereotypical gender roles, ultimately leaving gamers to ponder how they should understand the game'.[16] But detailed attention has not previously been paid to the role of Dante's Third Crusade backstory, nor how this setting informs the representation and evolution of his gender identity. I am not interested in issues of accuracy here, but rather in situating the game's story within existing tropes of crusading in general, and of the Third Crusade in particular.[17] Focusing on the game's content (rather than player responses to this), the following analysis gauges what these elements lend to the game. It begins with an outline of the crusading tropes which afford substance to the infrastructure of Dante's backstory. The significance of the siege and massacre at Acre as the game's narrative fulcrum is then explored, in order to demonstrate the implications for its construction of Dante's masculinity. Finally, it considers how the game reflects and adapts medieval understandings of what it means to be a man in its contrast of Dante with two other men: Alighiero, Dante's father, and Francesco.

## Crusading tropes

*Dante's Inferno* retains *Inferno's* main characters: Dante, Beatrice, and Virgil, and its rendition of the geography of Hell replicates Dante's vision exactly. The nine circles which he described are converted into nine levels through which Dante progresses. But the developers created their own plot overlaying this, in which Dante joins the Third Crusade alongside Beatrice's brother Francesco. Dante's violent, sinful conduct on crusade leads to the murder of Beatrice and his father; he returns home to find them freshly killed. Even worse, Beatrice's soul is abducted by Lucifer, who drags her down to Hell. Dante is compelled to follow and, with Virgil as his guide, fights his way through the nine circles/levels of Hell in order to rescue his beloved. In the process he is confronted with incidents from his past.

We witness Dante's past through a series of flashback cutscenes, which punctuate his campaign through Hell. The medium for this is the red fabric cross on Dante's chest; to a modern audience immediately recognisable as the classic visual signifier of a crusader.[18] The term 'crucesignatus' (bearer of the cross) was the term used in the Middle Ages to label an individual who had committed themself to one of the armed pilgrimages which we now call crusades.[19] From the First Crusade (1096–1100) onwards, those joining the enterprises proclaimed their vow by displaying a cross on their clothing.[20] Baldric of Bourgueil described how those who answered Urban II's 1095 call to rescue Jerusalem 'immediately sewed the sign of the holy cross onto their clothes'.[21] However, in the opening scene of the game we see, in graphic detail, Dante sewing a cloth cross, not onto his clothing but directly onto his naked chest, and howling in pain. Once the cross is in place we realise that it is like a tapestry, displaying images, and observe its role as a dynamic repository of Dante's memories. In this first instance the camera zooms in on an image of crusaders fighting Muslim forces which becomes a moving image, depicted first in stylised two-dimensional fashion, reminiscent of shadow puppets, then morphing into a more conventional strip cartoon animation. This same novel and engaging tactic is followed throughout the game.²² Level by level, viewing successive episodes from Dante's past, we discover that he has committed all the sins which circles two to nine embody: lust, gluttony, greed, anger, heresy, violence, fraud and treachery (circle one is Limbo). Progressing in chronological order Dante's full backstory gradually accretes through the brief cutscenes.

For example, in the Circle of Lust it is revealed that on the eve of Dante's departure for the crusade he made the following promise to Beatrice: 'By all that is holy, I vow to forsake all pleasures of the flesh until I return from this noble crusade.' Beatrice therefore agrees to have sex with Dante, even though they are not married, telling him: 'I gave myself to you because I know you will be faithful to our love.' But we discover that Dante breaks his vow. When guarding the prisoners at Acre he is unable to resist the temptation of a woman who offers to have sex with him in return for freeing her and her brother. Dante is immediately remorseful, saying, 'What have I done?' But it is too late. It transpires that Dante's betrayal of Beatrice is what placed her in Lucifer's clutches for, as Lucifer explains: 'She wagered her soul that you would be faithful. Her faith in you was very touching.' Cleopatra, who is the final boss in Lust, sums up the impact of Dante's lechery rather more candidly: 'You just gave up the keys to the Kingdom, and for what? The tits of a slave girl.' Furthermore, we discover that Dante's liaison with the female prisoner led to the murder of Beatrice and his father, for the 'brother' was actually the woman's husband, who subsequently sought out and killed Dante's family in revenge. The cutscenes include not only Dante's actions on crusade, but also moments from his childhood. For instance, in Gluttony we see Dante drinking excessively, with two women clinging lasciviously to him. Francesco knocks Dante's cup from his hand to stop him having a refill, and Dante angrily responds: 'Who made you a priest?' Then Dante transforms into a little boy and the camera pans back to reveal his father being plied with wine by two naked women. Alighiero, noticing Dante watching, throws up his arms angrily, using the same words: 'Who made you a priest?' As we exit the scene and return to Hell Lucifer says to Dante: 'Like father, like son.' Evidently aspects of Dante's immorality were learned from his father, a point we will explore at greater length below.

To return to Dante's chest cross, William Purkis has established that, for some medieval crusaders, bearing the cross encompassed more than stitching a cloth cross to their clothes. There are a number of surviving references from the late eleventh to the late fifteenth century of men formalising their commitment to a crusade by inscribing the cross directly onto their flesh.²³ He identifies this as a form of body modification whereby men would permanently scar themselves with the sign of the cross, either through branding or cutting.[24] It was a means of advertising the zealousness of their devotion to the crusading cause, by bearing the cross permanently on their bodies; an extreme expression of the perception that taking the cross was an act of mortification.[25] These medieval crusaders marked themselves with the cross before setting out, whereas Dante does it after he returns, yet still his act is analogous with meanings attached to medieval practices, for it is one of self-punishment. Additionally, his act makes manifest the idea that crusading was an experience which scarred men, not just physically, but mentally. Dante's experiences are literally written on his body, but only when he relives his memories via the cross does he fathom the terrible consequences of his rampant immorality, especially for those whom he loves: Beatrice and Francesco. As Steve Desilets, the lead designer, put it: 'The tapestry represents Dante's realisation that he needs to suffer for his sins, the same way that people have suffered by his hands.'[26]

The game's plot owes a good deal to generic motifs: a troubled, flawed protagonist motivated by the imperative to rescue his beautiful, imperilled sweetheart, thereby undertaking a journey of self-discovery as he comes to terms with his past. But, as the preceding discussion of Dante's chest cross demonstrates, it also draws on specifically medieval settings and ideas. Justin Lambros, Knight's co-writer and co-producer, noted that in the original poem Dante often faints and has to be carried by Virgil, saying: 'that's not a character we could use for a hero', implicitly because fainting (and indeed writing poetry) is deemed inherently unmanly.[27] Knight explained that the nature of the game required conflict and drama, dictating a central character who would fight through Hell, and have a clearly understandable motivation to do so.[28] Thus, Dante becomes a warrior, and given the chronological setting, from here it was a logical move to make him a crusader, *the* emblematic medieval warrior. As Elliott and Horswell explain:

> The distinctive assemblage of cross, warrior, armour and often helmet, sword and shield (also emblazoned with a red cross on white background) can function as a symbol of Christian militancy, unstoppable zeal, uncompromising purity, chivalric masculinity – or permutations of the above.[29]

Given perceptions of crusading as the ultimate expression of medieval martial manliness, turning Dante into a crusader is also an excellent fit for the stereotypical video game hero-protagonist. Dante's hypermasculinity is signalled by his exaggerated musculature, showcased further by the fact that he is essentially topless throughout the game.

In explaining 'the bold choice to give [Dante] a past as a crusader', Knight cited *Bram Stoker's Dracula* (1992) as an influence, noting that its director, Francis Ford Coppola:

> felt compelled to introduce this crusade narrative, where Dracula had this medieval past, where he's fighting in the Crusades. . . . And that was not part of Bram Stoker's novel, and, you know, that's one example that brings to mind how the Crusades have permeated culture . . . it's a modern idea that people continue to be interested in.[30]

Making Dante a crusader was therefore also a tactic for increasing the game's appeal. Popular interest in the crusades renders them a familiar setting for most gamers, in fact much more broadly familiar than the source poem *Inferno*. Commonplace perceptions both of the Middle Ages and the crusades also explain why a crusading backstory was judged by the developers as appropriate for a morally ambiguous protagonist. The first words we hear Dante speak in the game, just before he stitches the cross to his chest, are actually the first lines of the poem: 'At the midpoint on the journey of life, I found myself in a dark forest, for the clear path was lost.' Knight interpreted their significance thus: 'it's a metaphor for him being confused and troubled about his own life, but we wanted to go the nth degree for the video game and so we wanted him to basically have committed all these horrible sins'.[31] Crusading is generally condemned by modern commentators as a barbaric and immoral undertaking; indeed, the crusades are commonly regarded as a metonym for everything that was worst about the Middle Ages, perceived as brutal, backward, and bigoted.[32] *Dante's Inferno* is clearly predicated on this perspective.

The second cutscene shows the moment at which Dante joined the crusade. We see ranks of armed men standing outside a cathedral. The atmosphere is apocalyptic. A large fire burns before the cathedral, the dark sky is riven with lightning, and thunder rolls in the background as rain falls. In front of the cathedral stands a bishop, clad in robes and mitre of blood red. He addresses the men thus: 'Mercenaries of Florentina! In payment for taking the cross to reclaim the Holy Land your immaculate father hereby absolves you of all your sins!' The bishop thus offers a plenary indulgence: remission of sins for all those who fight for Christ. The indulgence was central to the crusades from the beginning; an aspect of crusading's status as an arduous, penitential act and a recognition of the self-sacrifice that being a crusader entailed.[33] However, to a modern audience the plenary indulgence usually signifies the greed and hypocrisy which motivated crusading, and which is often deemed to underpin the medieval church in general. An example of this view is provided by Ridley Scott's *Kingdom of Heaven* (2005) and is clearly conveyed by *Dante's Inferno* as well. The bishop's stature is unnaturally large, he almost fills the cathedral's central tympanum. As he speaks, we see a close-up which reveals that, despite wearing a v-shaped white tabard displaying the red cross, his appearance is thoroughly demonic. He grins malevolently, revealing pointed teeth, his nails are long and black, and one frontal shot appears to show him emerging from the fire. As he pronounces the absolution there's a quick glimpse of a woman shielding a baby and we hear a scream as blood spatters across the screen. His identification of the crowd as 'mercenaries' also immediately calls into question their motivations in joining the crusade, the implication being that their priority is material, rather than spiritual gains. A later cutscene shows an impressionistic precis of the crusading army's capture of Acre (which took place in July 1191). It is a frenetic scene of crusaders slaughtering Muslim forces in the midst of blood and flames, then celebrating over the impaled heads of their enemies. These sequences thus establish quickly and effectively the notion of the duplicitous, pitiless violence upon which crusading was based, aligning it with the modern perceptions outlined above.

The counterfeit nature of the bishop's absolution is established at the start of the game, when Dante is stabbed in the back, seemingly by the man who we later find out was the female prisoner's husband. Death comes to claim him and says: 'Dante, your fate is decided, everlasting damnation for your sins.' Dante replies: 'But that's not possible. The bishop assured us.' Later, Lucifer asks Dante: 'You think you're above reproach for your sins?' To which Dante replies: 'I took up the crusade. The bishop assured us that our sins would be absolved.' Lucifer mockingly retorts: 'And you believed him? You actually believed these salesmen of salvation?' Only in Hell does Dante grasp the Church's innate fraudulence and his own gullibility. Dante is also made to witness the murder of Beatrice and his father and comprehend that it was a direct consequence of his own actions. As Beatrice desperately flees we hear Lucifer's voice: 'Behold the slaughter and ruin of YOUR family, of YOUR home, of YOUR way of life', and, with that, Beatrice is impaled by the murderer's sword and falls to the ground. The implication is clear: the treatment which Dante meted out to the people of Acre was justly administered to him in return.[34] The game's depictions of the crusades render both comprehensible and plausible the sinfulness and duality with which Knight wanted to invest Dante. Dante's status as a crusader both inspired and enabled his moral transgressions, not only because of what he did on crusade, but because he wrongly believed that these actions had a holy justification.

Thus, *Dante's Inferno* fits into an established convention whereby crusading is not the main focus of the narrative, but an experiential backdrop suffusing the protagonist's subsequent character and actions, profoundly affecting those to whom he returns.³⁵ The choice of the Third Crusade for Dante's experiences is also narratively significant. The crusade which pitted Richard I against Saladin is the best known to modern audiences. This currency has its origins in the great popularity and influence of Walter Scott's novel *The Talisman* (1825), set during the Third Crusade.³⁶ The first *Assassin's Creed* (2007) also had a Third Crusade setting. The Third Crusade's familiarity derives much from its status as a standard element of modern retellings of Robin Hood. In *Robin and Marian* (1976), *Robin Hood: Prince of Thieves* (1991), *Robin Hood* (BBC TV 2006–2009), *Robin Hood* (2010), and *Robin Hood* (2018), Robin's experiences on the Third Crusade form the precursor to the main narrative.³⁷ Though never shown at length, we understand that what Robin does and witnesses on crusade affects him intensely, explaining subsequent aspects of his personality, accomplishments, and priorities. The trauma of being a crusader is often highlighted and making the Third Crusade a formative experience for Dante aligns his characterisation with this tradition. This sense of trauma is heightened by the recurring motif of Dante's encounters with his memories as a physically harrowing experience. Every cutscene is presaged by a moving or running Dante being brought up short and clutching his sides in pain, sometimes also dropping to his knees as the camera zooms in on the cross. Knight explained that as Dante re-encounters these past events 'we wanted them to be like nightmares'.³⁸ There are also connotations of PTSD here, as in some recent versions of Robin Hood.

## The massacre at Acre

Furthermore, the game interweaves Dante's past with the most notorious event of the Third Crusade: Richard I's massacre of over 2,000 Muslim prisoners outside Acre on 20 August 1191. The game opens with the following text, which is a reasonable precis of the historical circumstances:

> In the year 1191, European knights of the Third Crusade captured the city of Acre, about 30 miles from Jerusalem. Under orders from King Richard, 3,000 civilian prisoners were detained. They were held as ransom for a holy relic once taken by Saladin, the Kurdish protector of the Holy Land. As the hot summer wore on, Saladin dug in and refused to negotiate. Richard grew frustrated, unsure of an attack on Jerusalem. And the fate of the innocent prisoners was left undecided . . .

Then we cut to Dante in the dark forest, stitching the cross to his chest, which immediately intimates that 'the fate of the innocent prisoners' will play a central role in his story. The massacre at Acre is commonly deemed by both academic and popular assessments to be an egregious and inexcusably brutal act, even by medieval standards.[39] The game takes this position and the player is led to respond with revulsion, as highlighted by the focus on a kneeling woman holding a baby when first dramatising the massacre during the opening cutscene. This is the same woman who later reappears during the bishop's address, discussed above. Significantly a parallel tactic was employed in Ridley Scott's *Robin Hood*, which, like *Dante's Inferno* was released in 2010. Although the massacre itself is not shown, it is referenced by Robin Hood (played by Russell Crowe) in an exchange with Richard I:

> When you had us herd two and a half thousand Muslim men, women and children together; the young woman at my feet, with her hands bound, she looked up at me. There wasn't fear in her eyes, there wasn't anger. There was only pity. She knew that when you gave the order, and our blades would descend upon their heads, that in that moment we would be godless. All of us. Godless.

The inclusion of reference to the massacre may have been influenced by *Robin and Marian* in which, similarly, the massacre itself is not shown. But Robin (Sean Connery) relates it to Marian (Audrey Hepburn) in shocking terms, underlining that Richard's primary motivation was greed and emphasising the sheer contempt with which the Muslims were held by the crusaders. Thus, in *Dante's Inferno*, as in these two films, the massacre at Acre is shorthand for the utterly savage and morally debased nature of crusading.

Significantly, the massacre is commonly interpreted as a product of Richard's prodigious anger. Stephen J. Spencer demonstrates that the claim Richard ordered the executions while overwhelmed by a fit of rage appears frequently in modern scholarship. This despite the fact that very few contemporary chroniclers actually attributed the event to Richard's untrammelled ire.[40] But the game relieves Richard of blame entirely. We first see the massacre briefly in the opening scenes of the game, but without knowing how or why it began. Gradually cutscenes build to the shocking revelation that Dante himself instigated the atrocity. In the Circle of Anger, significantly, we pan through a bloody, burning valley crowded with chained prisoners. The words 'your immaculate father hereby absolves you' are heard as the huge, monstrous bishop briefly reappears. As he dissolves Dante says: 'We came here to kill these heretics!' To which Francesco retorts: 'We came to reclaim the Holy Land.' Dante turns, furious: 'Since when are heretics worth a Christian life?' The scene ends as he raises his sword above his head shouting 'Enough!' and then brings it down towards the prisoners as

Francesco tries to restrain him. This scene is continued in the Circle of Violence, with Dante continuing to shout 'Enough!' at Francesco, who parries Dante's sword with his own, shouting: 'No! It is not for us to decide the fate of these souls!' Dante, raging, exclaims: 'What souls?! THAT is why we fight! They are not us!' He begins to butcher the prisoners, declaiming: 'Fight with me crusaders! Spill the blood of heathens! There is no shame! Their souls are already lost!' As the bloody scene ends, a great flaming, horned demon appears in the background, with a nasty grin.

Thus, Richard's signature excessive rage and its status as the cause of the massacre is transposed to Dante, whose anger has its origins in religious prejudice. Richard himself is appalled, appearing briefly in the aftermath to demand: 'God in Heaven! Who is responsible for this?' Here Richard's anger is inspired *by* the massacre, it is not the inspiration *for* the massacre. Attributing the massacre to rage (whether Richard's or Dante's) chimes with the argument that anger was the overriding emotion of crusading, and that this explains the levels of violence attendant on certain key episodes (such as this, and the sack of Jerusalem in 1099).[41] Certainly, the cutscenes provide incontrovertible proof of the pernicious nature of crusading, which, as we have seen, the game establishes from the start. Moreover, they explain to the player why Dante deserved to go to Hell. This is made clear by Knight's account of why he chose the massacre at Acre as the pivotal event of Dante's backstory:

> Well I was compelled by this one particular historical event in the Third Crusade [Knight briefly recounts the circumstances of the massacre]. And, to me, that was a really interesting historical moment, and as we look for a way to craft the path of our Dante, and sort-of reimagine him as this guy who has gone through a lot of really morally questionable activities, that felt like kind-of a really powerful hotbed of bad choices, and was thematically appropriate. [We] made him part of that event . . . we played with the timeline a little bit, and it provides kind-of the right backstory for our guy.[42]

Knight does not explicitly mention the commonplace connection between Richard's anger and the massacre, but given the game's depiction of the event and the emphasis placed on Dante's growing, uncontrollable fury in the cutscenes, it seems likely that this tradition was an influencing factor. Spencer traces in detail the essential role played by Richard's conduct on the Third Crusade (especially at Acre) in forming modern appraisals of his temperament and thus character.[43] As Spencer puts it, several influential modern scholars have made 'a cognitive connection between the execution – interpreted as an unusually brutal event – and Richard's dysfunctional temperament'.[44] The logic of such evaluations proceeds as follows: Richard's inability to moderate his anger reveals that he was emotionally unstable, leading to his unwarranted aggression and violence.

## Adapting medieval and crusader masculinities

To build on Spencer's contention, the massacre, interpreted in this fashion, is therefore also revelatory of Richard's dysfunctional gender identity, because the exercise of self-mastery was indispensable to medieval definitions of masculinity. Prescriptions of ideal masculinity repeatedly assert that a man should possess the physical, intellectual, and moral strength to suppress sinful bodily appetites and urges of various kinds: lust, gluttony, avarice, also anger, fear, self-interest, and so on. It was all the more important that a ruler/leader should exercise self-mastery, for this essential attribute qualified him to wield authority over others.[45] As the game replaces Richard with Dante, this gendered reading also applies to Dante, and is intimated by the brief synopsis of the plot included in the game's insert, which states: 'Dante's passions consume him as he gives in to the darkness.'

Moreover, this gender specific definition of virtue was also an essential attribute of the crusader's identity. As crusading was formalised, the commitment signified by the cloth cross was also articulated in the form of crusading vows. These varied in precise form but usually included elements of abstinence in relation to sex and diet, as befitted one who was undertaking a form of pilgrimage.[46] The vow was linked to the notion of crusading as a penitential act, and also entitled the crusader to various legal and spiritual privileges. But if the vow was broken, or not fulfilled, the penalty was excommunication. The devout and moral quality of a crusading force was deemed to be as vital to its success as the military quality, for this was a means of ensuring divine support. In particular, both canon lawyers and chroniclers routinely attributed military defeats to the sexual improprieties of crusaders, who had thus earned God's disapprobation.[47] Thus, when Dante has sex with the female prisoner he breaks both his vow to Beatrice, and his vow as a crusader. Hence the pivotal status of the massacre within the game. Just as the massacre has been employed as a register for Richard's character and a means of demonstrating his defective nature, so it functions within the game for Dante. The narrative of the cutscenes positions the massacre as the culmination of Dante's progressive degeneration. It is the moment of Dante's final and absolute surrender to bodily urges, hypocritically indulged under cover of papal authorisation. Fundamentally, the game hinges on Dante's status as a man. This is highlighted by the very first cutscene in which we see Dante walk past the prisoners as a woman's voice calls out to him: 'What kind of man locks up helpless women? There will be a day of reckoning crusader.' When Beatrice confronts Dante with his betrayal of her, saying: 'You broke your promise', Dante tries to defend himself, replying: 'You don't know what it was like', but Lucifer points out that she does know: 'I showed her.' The implication is that the crusade was a disturbing experience for Dante, yet he should have been able to surmount temptations and curb his passions. Instead the cutscenes reveal the extent of his depravity, he has transgressed virtuous norms, which serve to emasculate him. Dante's passage through Hell thus constitutes the recovery of his vitiated masculinity as he comprehends and accepts his culpability.

This is a gradual process, however. In addition to citing the indulgence as authorisation for his actions, Dante also attempts to abnegate responsibility on the grounds of nurture. As we saw earlier, the cutscene in Gluttony, and Lucifer's commentary on it, signal that the origins of Dante's sinfulness lie with his father, Alighiero. This is further elaborated by the cutscene in the Circle of Greed (greed in the sense of avarice). We see Alighiero taking sacks of produce from a peasant family. When their father asks: 'How will I feed my family?' Alighiero gives a cruel smile, replying: 'That's not my problem. I have friends to entertain.' We then see Alighiero at the centre of a riotous banquet, with plentiful food and drink, and voluptuous serving women. Young Dante appears in the foreground, clearly enjoying what he sees, to judge by his sinister smile. Then he transforms into a horned devil. This conveys that Dante was corrupted by his upbringing; an environment which normalised greedy, gluttonous, lustful and self-interested behaviour. A later cutscene confirms this in tragic terms. To Dante's horror, he encounters his mother in the Wood of Suicides (part of the Circle of Violence). He had been led to believe by his father that she had died of a fever. However, his mother explains that she hanged herself because: 'I despised your father's cruelty. But I was too weak to defy him. And so – I took my own life. And you. You learned his ways.' So Dante is implicated in her death too. His mother could not face seeing him grow up to become a rapacious, dissipated, and destructive reprobate like his father.[48]

Alighiero is, unsurprisingly, in Hell himself; the final boss of the Circle of Greed, his body gross and distended, festooned with heavy gold chains. When the two encounter each other Alighiero says: 'So! You think you're a better man than your father?' To which Dante replies: 'I think I'm too much the same man as my father.' After a further exchange Dante's father says: 'Then we'll find out who's the better man.' During the fight Alighiero variously questions his son's masculinity: 'Come on! Be a man! . . . I'm ashamed of you! . . . You're half a man! . . . All this for a woman?! . . . Are you man enough for this?' The fight between the two highlights two contrasting versions of masculinity: Alighiero's self-aggrandising hypermasculinity of combat to decide who is dominant versus Dante's controlled use of violence to achieve an end which benefits others.[49] After Dante defeats his father they have a final exchange in a cutscene, where Alighiero says: 'Go on . . . use me as an excuse. Blame me for everything.' Dante says: 'You're so full of greed and hate. Is that all you had to offer me?' But Alighiero retorts: 'I'm not responsible for the man you are.' Dante replies: 'And I will not be damned like you!' and absolves him. Dante may have been brought up by a dissolute father who drove his mother to suicide, but he was not doomed to become the same sort of man, as his father's final words confirm. Dante had free will, and could have behaved virtuously. This illustrates one of the central themes of the game, as Knight explained: 'You choose to sin or not to sin . . . it's hard to be holy but the reward is much greater!'[50] The fact that Dante chose to sin, to revel in pleasure and violence rather than exercise restraint, is an unequivocal symptom of his flawed masculinity.

Another tactic which the game utilises to assert the deficiency of Dante's masculinity is the depiction of Francesco as a principled counterpart. Introducing Francesco, the game's insert states:

> He joined Dante on the Crusades and fought bravely by his side. Francesco's actions, however, differed greatly from Dante's. During his time in the Crusades, Francesco was the nobler and more virtuous of the two. Francesco was a good man who only joined the Crusades in hopes of reclaiming the holy city of Jerusalem.

Although the game establishes crusading as reprehensible, Francesco is more honourable because he at least took the cross purely for spiritual reasons. Whereas Dante used the crusade as an opportunity to indulge his appetites, secure in the bishop's promise of absolution. Significantly, Francesco questions the indulgence in a cutscene which shows the crowd of men listening to the bishop, with repetition of his words 'your immaculate father hereby absolves you of all your sins!'. Francesco asks: 'Is it true he can absolve our sins without confession?' To which Dante replies: 'Would a bishop lie?' As we have seen, Francesco also tries to restrain Dante's immorality, even attempting to save the prisoners. Francesco thus embodies chivalric masculinity, not only because of his personal virtue, but because he uses his strength to try and protect others. As we have seen, it is in the Circle of Violence that Dante is identified as the ringleader of the massacre. This cutscene plays in an area called 'The Abominable Sands' which Virgil tells Dante is where those who have committed violence against God are punished. It is a recreation of the crusades setting we see in the cutscenes, complete with zombie crusader mobs, implicitly those who fought alongside Dante. Francesco is the final boss of this level, rendered with a monstrous body, semi-flayed, still wearing his crusader tabard, his back impaled by several swords. As Dante fights him, Francesco makes a number of accusatory denouncements, which, like Alighiero's, question Dante's manhood: 'You. YOU did this to me! . . . You don't deserve to be my sister's slave, let alone her lord. . . . Come on, coward! . . . I begged you not to do it! . . . You started the killing! . . . You fell for a bishop's lie! . . . You're foolish as ever! . . . God has turned against you.' Once Francesco is defeated he addresses Dante in a cutscene: 'Our deeds were done in the name of God. Why has he forsaken us?' Dante, having by now grasped the true nature of the crusade replies: 'In the name of God? Murder is only in the name of the murderer.'

However, Dante still does not seem to understand why Francesco attacked him, although the swords in his back are suggestive. It was established earlier in the game that as well as swearing to be chaste and faithful to Beatrice, Dante also promised her: 'I will protect your brother like he is my own.' But Dante broke this promise too. The penultimate circle/level is Fraud, constituting a series of ten combat challenges, a counterpart to the ten 'malebolge' ('evil ditches') described by Dante in *Inferno*. Having overcome these Dante encounters Beatrice and pleads with her: 'Beatrice, stop this. I have faced all of my sins, and I am ready to take you home.' She replies, disdainfully: 'All your sins? I think not. Look into the Ninth Circle of Hell. Look into the dark, cold realm of the Traitors.' This presages the final cutscene, which discloses the aftermath of the massacre. Dante is covered in blood, standing knee deep in corpses, exhausted by the slaughter. This is the moment at which Richard expresses his horror, quoted above. In response to Richard's demand to know who is responsible, Francesco steps forward, having asked Dante to take care of Beatrice, and declares: 'I am responsible.' Francesco is seized by armed men and Richard orders that he be hanged. Dante remains silent, and then rides at pace out of the city. As he leaves we hear his voiceover: 'Beatrice . . . I will protect you', but as these words are spoken, the riding Dante transforms into the man who will murder her. Thus, the untarnished Francesco bravely accepts the punishment which Dante should have suffered. Like his sister, Beatrice, he is an innocent who dies because of Dante's inability to control himself. By contrast Dante is a coward whose craven failure to own up to the massacre is physically embodied by the swords piercing Francesco: Dante figuratively stabs him in the back.[51] The betrayal of Francesco is thus affirmed as the most heinous of Dante's sins. Dante has violated the ties and obligations not just of love, but of brotherhood, and this provides final, categorical confirmation of his abject lack of manliness.

Such is the magnitude of Dante's betrayal of Francesco that this is the point at which Dante finally concedes. As the cutscene ends, Beatrice challenges Dante: 'You condemned my brother to death for YOUR crime. What is your answer for this treachery?' Dante falls to his knees: 'None. I give up on this journey. My place is here, in Hell, and yours is in Paradise. I am truly sorry for what I have done. May you one day forgive me.' This confessional moment then becomes one of triumph and revivification. Beatrice is released and borne up to Heaven by an angel, who reassures Dante that he will see her again. Dante now embodies virtue and is thereby empowered to defeat Lucifer, the final boss. Dante believes himself to be on a quest to rescue Beatrice, but, in fact, he rescues himself. As Knight observes: 'So it really does become less of a rescue mission, more of a redemption story.'[52] Lucifer reveals to Dante that when he was stabbed and Death came to claim him, he had actually died, and thus is trapped in Hell. But the redemption signalled by Dante's conquest of Lucifer enables him to escape Hell. It also strips him of his crusader apparel; his sins forgiven, he emerges naked into Purgatory. Dante's nudity signifies innocence, and the purging of his gendered transgressions is also indicated by the scorched remains of the cross on his chest, which he tears off and discards. *Dante's Inferno* dramatises the recuperation of Dante's masculinity via a pilgrimage of self-discovery. The process of combating embodiments of the sins he committed, and confronting those he has wronged leads Dante to understand and repent the extent of his weaknesses, his crimes, and their repercussions. Thus, his manhood is restored.

## Conclusion

*Dante's Inferno* offers a compelling rendition of certain commonplace perceptions of crusading, using these to dramatise the destructive effects of rampant masculinity both on Dante's victims, and on Dante himself. Dante's passage through Hell teaches him that true manhood lies in surmounting, not indulging his passions, and that manhood is consequently the route to salvation. Indeed, the gendered dimensions of the narrative and their interleaving with crusading tropes arguably present an authentic expression of certain medieval ideas about what it means to be a man, and the ways in which masculinity can be both lost and recovered. However, that narrative is embedded in a medium designed, fundamentally, to be entertaining. In this type of game that means offering players multiple inventive opportunities to assault, eviscerate, and dismember mobs, as well as a good deal of nudity (mostly, although not exclusively, female nudity). Knight justified the nudity as: 'appropriate to the subject matter. If you look at any painting of hell, everybody's naked. . . . We try not to do anything that wasn't appropriate to the material, but it's definitely mature content.'[53] Certainly the creators of *Dante's Inferno* were at pains to produce a game which would be a worthy addition to the tradition of reimagining Dante's *Inferno*.[54] Interviews with Knight and others articulate the hope that the game would provoke reflection on issues of morality. In discussing the highly sexualised environment and mobs created for the Circle of Lust, art director Ash Huang stated: 'you can be totally gratuitous and really kind-of like silly about it and really pornographic about it, you know, let's just hang a huge penis out there, you know, and call it a day! You can also make it kind-of interesting, thoughtful, provocative.'[55] There is thus a good deal of evidence for the nuanced framing which the creators devised for the game. Although it has to be said that these efforts were rather undercut by aspects of the game's marketing campaign, especially the 'Sin to Win' promotion at Comic Con 2009, widely condemned as sexist and as promoting sexual harassment.[56]

Nonetheless, progressive interpretations of *Dante's Inferno*, which read the depiction of Dante's hypermasculinity as an invitation to question the gender stereotypes inherent to certain types of game, are valid.[57] *Dante's Inferno* does offer a critique both of toxic masculinity and of the crusading ideologies which enabled his atrocities. Yet Dante remains an avatar of unabashedly violent medieval manhood. This is all the more problematic because of the frequency with which the medieval knight, especially the medieval crusader knight, is currently brought into the service of reactionary and extremist ideologies, in particular of white supremacy.[58] The issue of player responses to and appropriations of *Dante's Inferno* is certainly worthy of greater attention than I am able to give it here. In 2019 a Reddit user posted an anonymised Facebook post reading: 'The Crusades were a defensive war in response to centuries of Islamic jihad against Europe', which has become a standard far-right 'take' on the crusades.[59] This claim was illustrated by a still from a *Dante's Inferno* cutscene, showing Dante and other crusaders in classic pose, kneeling with hands resting on the hilts of their unsheathed swords. The post was made in a group called 'Insane People Facebook', indicating the Reddit user's opinion of its message. Moreover, the first commenter asked: 'Aside from the idiocy of the post, I'm just curious where the background art's from?' Another user identified either the game or film of *Dante's Inferno* as the source (it is actually from the game), noting: 'What's ironic is that the message that both TRY to display is that fighting/war is bad, and the crusades were a travesty.'

The creators intended that players should take certain meanings away from *Dante's Inferno*. They took steps to try and direct players' interpretations accordingly, in the way the narrative is constructed, in the game's supporting materials, and in extensive pre-release interviews. But an individual player's understanding of the game will usually be determined more significantly by their pre-existing views, formed by aspects of their own identity and environment. Gary Blackburn and Erica Scharrer's research indicates that young adults (both men and women) who favour playing violent video games (such as *Dante's Inferno*) generally endorse highly traditional forms of hypermasculinity.[60] Moreover, Nicholas Taylor and Gerald Vorhees highlight 'the inextricable and numerous ways in which games have historically served (and continue to serve) neo-colonial white-supremacist capitalist patriarchy'.[61] Thus, analysing the intertwined configurations of crusading and masculinity presented by *Dante's Inferno* is important as evidence for modern perceptions of crusading, and of what it meant to be a man in the Middle Ages. Such analysis is also important for what it reveals about modern ideologies of masculinity and the troubling tenacity of toxic masculinity even within narratives which make some attempt to dismantle it.

## Notes

1 I am very grateful to Robert Houghton and Mike Horswell for their insightful comments on drafts of this essay.
2 *Crusading and Masculinities*, ed. Natasha R. Hodgson, Katherine J. Lewis, and Matthew M. Mesley (London and New York, NY: Routledge, 2019); Andrew B. R. Elliott and Mike Horswell, "Crusading Icons: Medievalism and Authenticity in Historical Digital Games," in *History in Games: Contingencies of an Authentic Past*, ed. Martin Lorber and Felix Zimmermann (Bielefeld: transcript Verlag, 2020).
3 Elliott and Horswell, "Crusading Icons," 5; Louise D'Arcens, "The Crusades and Medievalism," in *The Cambridge Companion to the Literature of the Crusades*, ed. Anthony Bale (Cambridge: Cambridge University Press, 2019), 248–62.
4 E.g. "*Dante's Inferno* Interview: Jonathan Knight, Executive Producer," *x360aNews* (from November 2009), www.youtube.com/watch?v=AsZkO4O bPlU, accessed August 18, 2020.
5 An accompanying anime feature film of the game's story was also released.

6 I am very grateful to my husband, Graeme Neath, for playing through the game with me and discussing the ideas contained in this chapter.
7 For a collation of reviews: "*Dante's Inferno* (video game)," https://en.wikipedia.org/wiki/Dante%27s_Inferno_(video_game), accessed August 18, 2020.
8 E.g. Christopher Grant, "*Dante's Inferno*: The Book Based on the Game, Based on the Poem, Based on the Theology," www.engadget.com/2010-02-02-dantes-inferno-the-book-based-on-the-game-based-on-the-poem-ba.html, accessed August 18, 2020. See also Bruno Lessard, "The Game's Two Bodies, Or The Fate of *Figura* in *Dante's Inferno*," in *Digital Gaming Re-imagines the Middle Ages*, ed. Daniel T. Kline (London: Routledge, 2014), 133, 146.
9 These pages were subsequently removed but can still be partially accessed via the Wayback Machine on: archive.org.
10 *Dante's Inferno*, trans. Henry Wadsworth Longfellow (New York, NY: Del Rey, 2010).
11 Ibid.; Knight, "Introduction," xvii–xviii.
12 Brandon K. Essary, "Dante's '*Inferno*', Video Games, and Pop Pedagogy," *Parole Rubate: Rivista Internazionale Di Studi Sulla Citazione* 20 (2019): 59–82. With thanks to David Bowe for this reference. See also Angela Jane Weisl and Kevin J. Stevens, "The Middle Ages in the Depths of Hell: Pedagogical Possibility and the Past in *Dante's Inferno*," in *Digital Gaming*, ed. Daniel T. Kline (London: Routledge, 2014).
13 "*Dante's Inferno*: Full Walkthrough," Gamer's Little Playground, www.youtube.com/watch?v=PcMS95fYZ30, accessed August 18, 2020.
14 Oliver Chadwick, "Courtly Violence, Digital Play: Adapting Medieval Courtly Masculinities in *Dante's Inferno*," in *Digital Gaming*, ed. Daniel T. Kline (London: Routledge, 2014), 149 (emphasis in original).
15 Ibid., 153–58.
16 Denise A. Ayo, "When Did Dante Become a Scythe-Wielding Badass? Modelling Adaptation and Shifting Gender Convention in *Dante's Inferno*," in *Game On, Hollywood! Essays on the Intersection of Video Games and Cinema*, ed. Gretchen Papazian and Joseph Michael Sommers (Jefferson, NC: McFarland, 2013), 111. For further analysis of Dante's body: Timothy J. Walsh and John T. Sebastian, "Shades of Dante: Virtual Bodies in *Dante's Inferno*," in *Digital Gaming*, ed. Daniel T. Kline (London: Routledge, 2014).
17 For the redundancy of the "accuracy" approach: Matthew Wilhelm Kapell and Andrew B. R. Elliott, eds., *Playing with the Past: Digital Games and the Simulation of History* (New York, NY: Bloomsbury, 2013).
18 Elliott and Horswell, "Crusading Icons," 9.
19 William J. Purkis, "'Zealous Imitation': The Materiality of the Crusader's Marked Body," *Material Religion* 14, no. 4 (2018): 440.
20 William J. Purkis, *Crusading Spirituality in the Holy Land and Iberia, c. 1095–c. 1187* (Woodbridge: The Boydell Press, 2014), 30–39.
21 Ibid., 33.
22 For more detailed discussion see Lorenzo Servitje, "Digital Mortification of Literary Flesh: Computational Logistics and Violences of Remediation in Visceral Games' *Dante's Inferno*," *Games and Culture* 9, no. 5 (2014): 377–81.
23 Purkis, "'Zealous Imitation'," passim.
24 Ibid., 441.
25 Ibid., 447–49.

26 "*Dante's Inferno*, Developer Diary 4," *Game*, www.youtube.com/watch?v=5eEPw5BArv0, accessed August 18, 2020.
27 Ibid.
28 "*Dante's Inferno* Interview: Jonathan Knight."
29 Elliott and Horswell, "Crusading Icons," 9. For the persistent appeal of military masculinity in games more generally see Gregory Blackburn, "Army Men: Military Masculinity in *Call of Duty*," and Aaron Trammell, "Militarism and Masculinity in *Dungeons & Dragons*," both in *Masculinities in Play*, ed. Nicholas Taylor and Gerald Vorhees (Cham: Palgrave MacMillan, 2018).
30 Christian Nutt, "The Road to Hell: The Creative Direction of *Dante's Inferno*," www.gamasutra.com/view/feature/4266/the_road_to_hell_the_creative_.php?print=1, accessed August 18, 2020.
31 "*Dante's Inferno*, Developer Diary 4."
32 D'Arcens, "Crusades and Medievalism," 258–59.
33 Ane L. Bysted, *The Crusade Indulgence: Spiritual Rewards and the Theology of the Crusades, c. 1095–1216* (Leiden: Brill, 2014).
34 Servitje reads into the game an anti-war critique directed at Western military interventions in Iraq and Afghanistan, "Computational Logistics," 382.
35 Elizabeth Siberry, "The Crusader's Departure and Return: A Much later Perspective," in *Gendering the Crusades*, ed. Susan B. Edgington and Sarah Lambert (Cardiff: University of Wales Press, 2001).
36 Elizabeth Siberry, *The New Crusaders: Images of the Crusades in the 19th and Early 20th Centuries* (Aldershot: Ashgate, 2000), 112–20.
37 Stephen Knight, "Robin Hood and the Crusades: When and Why Did the Longbowman of the People Mount Up Like a Lord?" *Florilegium* 23, no. 1 (2006); Rob Gossedge, "'We Are Robin Hood': The Outlaw Tradition in Contemporary Popular Culture," in *Medieval Afterlives in Contemporary Culture*, ed. Gail Ashton (London: Bloomsbury, 2015).
38 "*Dante's Inferno*, Developer Diary 4."
39 Stephen J. Spencer, "'Like a Raging Lion': Richard the Lionheart's Anger during the Third Crusade in Medieval and Modern Historiography," *English Historical Review* 556 (2017).
40 Ibid., 504–11.
41 Sophia Menache, "Love of God, or Hatred of Your Enemy?" The Emotional Voices of the Crusades," *Mirabilia* 10 (2010); Spencer, "Like a Raging Lion," 522.
42 Nutt, "The Road to Hell."
43 Spencer, "Like a Raging Lion," 497 and passim.
44 Ibid., 521.
45 Katherine J. Lewis, *Kingship and Masculinity in Late Medieval England* (London and New York, NY: Routledge, 2013), 22–30.
46 James A. Brundage, "The Votive Obligations of Crusaders: The Development of a Canonistic Doctrine," *Traditio* 24 (1968).
47 Natasha R. Hodgson, *Women, Crusading and the Holy Land in Historical Narrative* (Woodbridge: The Boydell Press, 2007), 135–39.
48 The anime feature film takes this further: young Dante witnesses his father beating his mother.
49 I owe this observation to Mike Horswell.

50 "*Dante's Inferno*, Developer Diary 6," *ElectronicElation*, www.youtube.com/watch?v=jwY25ImJGZ8, accessed August 18, 2020.
51 That the swords in Francesco's back were designed to be read in this way was discussed by combat designer John Swisshelm, "*Dante's Inferno*, Developer Diary 7," *ElectronicElation*, www.youtube.com/watch?v=WYO-BTymGNw, accessed August 18, 2020.
52 Nutt, "The Road to Hell."
53 Matt Casamassina, "*Dante's Inferno* Interview," www.ign.com/articles/2010/02/03/dantes-inferno-interview, accessed August 18, 2020.
54 Knight, "Introduction."
55 "*Dante's Inferno*, Developer Diary 2," *Game*, www.youtube.com/watch?v=9VghmLoQKpw, accessed August 18, 2020.
56 "EA Booth Babe Bounty," https://geekfeminism.wikia.org/wiki/EA_booth_babe_bounty, accessed August 18, 2020.
57 Ayo, "When Did Dante," 109–10.
58 Laurie Finke and Martin B. Shichtman, "Who's Your Daddy? New Age Grails," *Arthuriana* 19, no. 3 (2009); Andrew B. R. Elliott, *Medievalism, Politics and Mass Media: Appropriating the Middle Ages in the Twenty-First Century* (Cambridge: D. S. Brewer, 2017).
59 "The More You Know," www.reddit.com/r/insanepeoplefacebook/comments/bgqwsb/the_more_you_know/, accessed August 18, 2020; Kristin Skottki, "The Dead, the Revived and the Recreated Pasts: 'Structural Amnesia' in Representations of Crusade History," in *Perceptions of the Crusades from the Nineteenth to the Twenty-First Century: Engaging the Crusades, Volume One*, ed. Mike Horswell and Jonathan Phillips (Abingdon: Routledge, 2018), 121–24.
60 Gary Blackburn and Erica Scharrer, "Video Game Playing and Beliefs About Masculinity Among Male and Female Emerging Adults", *Sex Roles* 80 (5–6) (2019).
61 Nicholas Taylor and Gerald Vorhees, "Introduction: Masculinity and Gaming: Mediated Masculinities in Play," in *Masculinities in Play*, ed. Nicholas Taylor and Gerald Vorhees (Cham: Palgrave MacMillan, 2018), 1.

## Bibliography

Ayo, Denise A. "When Did Dante Become a Scythe-Wielding Badass? Modelling Adaptation and Shifting Gender Convention in *Dante's Inferno*." In *Game On, Hollywood! Essays on the Intersection of Video Games and Cinema*, edited by Gretchen Papazian and Joseph Michael Sommers, 101–14. Jefferson, NC: McFarland, 2013.

Blackburn, Gregory. "Army Men: Military Masculinity in *Call of Duty*." In *Masculinities in Play*, edited by Nicholas Taylor and Gerald Vorhees, 37–54. Cham: Palgrave Macmillan, 2018.

Blackburn, Gary, and Erica Scharrer, "Video Game Playing and Beliefs About Masculinity Among Male and Female Emerging Adults", *Sex Roles* 80 (5–6) (2019), 310–24.

Brundage, James A. "The Votive Obligations of Crusaders: The Development of a Canonistic Doctrine." *Traditio* 24 (1968): 77–118.

Bysted, Ane L. *The Crusade Indulgence: Spiritual Rewards and the Theology of the Crusades, c. 1095–1216*. Leiden: Brill, 2014.

Casamassina, Matt. "*Dante's Inferno* Interview." www.ign.com/articles/2010/02/03/dantes-inferno-interview. Accessed August 18, 2020.

Chadwick, Oliver. "Courtly Violence, Digital Play: Adapting Medieval Courtly Masculinities in *Dante's Inferno*." In *Digital Gaming Re-imagines the Middle Ages*, edited by Daniel T. Kline, 148–61. London: Routledge, 2014.

*Dante's Inferno*, trans. Henry Wadsworth Longfellow. New York, NY: Del Rey, 2010.

"*Dante's Inferno*, Developer Diary 2." Game. www.youtube.com/watch?v=9VghmLoQKpw. Accessed August 18, 2020.

"*Dante's Inferno*, Developer Diary 4." Game. www.youtube.com/watch?v=5eEPw5BArv0. Accessed August 18, 2020.

"*Dante's Inferno*, Developer Diary 6." ElectronicElation. www.youtube.com/watch?v=jwY25ImJGZ8. Accessed August 18, 2020.

"*Dante's Inferno*, Developer Diary 7." ElectronicElation. www.youtube.com/watch?v=WYO-BTymGNw. Accessed August 18, 2020.

"*Dante's Inferno*: Full Walkthrough." Gamer's Little Playground. www.youtube.com/watch?v=PcMS95fYZ30. Accessed August 18, 2020.

"*Dante's Inferno* Interview: Jonathan Knight, Executive Producer." x360aNews (from November 2009). www.youtube.com/watch?v=AsZkO4ObPlU. Accessed August 18, 2020.

"*Dante's Inferno* (video game)." https://en.wikipedia.org/wiki/Dante%27s_Inferno_(video_game). Accessed August 18, 2020.

D'Arcens, Louise. "The Crusades and Medievalism." In *The Cambridge Companion to the Literature of the Crusades*, edited by Anthony Bale, 248–62. Cambridge: Cambridge University Press, 2019.

"EA Booth Babe Bounty." https://geekfeminism.wikia.org/wiki/EA_booth_babe_bounty. Accessed August 18, 2020.

Elliott, Andrew B. R. *Medievalism, Politics and Mass Media: Appropriating the Middle Ages in the Twenty-First Century*. Cambridge: D.S. Brewer, 2017.

Elliott, Andrew B. R., and Mike Horswell. "Crusading Icons: Medievalism and Authenticity in Historical Digital Games." In *History in Games: Contingencies of an Authentic Past*, edited by Martin Lorber and Felix Zimmermann, 137–156. Bielefeld: transcript Verlag, 2020.

Essary, Brandon K. "Dante's '*Inferno*', Video Games, and Pop Pedagogy." *Parole Rubate: Rivista Internazionale Di Studi Sulla Citazione* 20 (2019): 59–82.

Finke, Laurie, and Martin B. Shichtman. "Who's Your Daddy? New Age Grails." *Arthuriana* 19, no. 3 (2009): 25–33.

Gossedge, Rob. "'We Are Robin Hood': The Outlaw Tradition in Contemporary Popular Culture." In *Medieval Afterlives in Contemporary Culture*, edited by Gail Ashton, 251–62. London: Bloomsbury, 2015.

Grant, Christopher. "*Dante's Inferno*: The Book Based on the Game, Based on the Poem, Based on the Theology." www.engadget.com/2010-02-02-dantes-inferno-the-book-based-on-the-game-based-on-the-poem-ba.html. Accessed August 18, 2020.

Hodgson, Natasha R. *Women, Crusading and the Holy Land in Historical Narrative*. Woodbridge: The Boydell Press, 2007.

Hodgson, Natasha R., Katherine J. Lewis, and Matthew M. Mesley, eds. *Crusading and Masculinities*. London: Routledge, 2019.

Kapell, Matthew Wilhelm, and Andrew B. R. Elliott, eds. *Playing with the Past: Digital Games and the Simulation of History*. New York, NY: Bloomsbury, 2013.

Knight, Stephen. "Robin Hood and the Crusades: When and Why Did the Longbowman of the People Mount Up Like a Lord?" *Florilegium* 23, no. 1 (2006): 201–22.

Lessard, Bruno. "The Game's Two Bodies, or the Fate of *Figura* in *Dante's Inferno*." In *Digital Gaming Re-imagines the Middle Ages*, edited by Daniel T. Kline, 133–47. London: Routledge, 2014.

Lewis, Katherine J. *Kingship and Masculinity in Late Medieval England*. London: Routledge, 2013.

Menache, Sophia. "'Love of God, or Hatred of Your Enemy?' The Emotional Voices of the Crusades." *Mirabilia* 10 (2010): 1–20.

Purkis, William J. *Crusading Spirituality in the Holy Land and Iberia, c. 1095– c. 1187*. Woodbridge: The Boydell Press, 2014.

———. "'Zealous Imitation': The Materiality of the Crusader's Marked Body." *Material Religion* 14, no. 4 (2018): 438–53.

Servitje, Lorenzo. "Digital Mortification of Literary Flesh: Computational Logistics and Violences of Remediation in Visceral Games' *Dante's Inferno*." *Games and Culture* 9, no. 5 (2014): 368–88.

Siberry, Elizabeth. "The Crusader's Departure and Return: A Much later Perspective." In *Gendering the Crusades*, edited by Susan B. Edgington and Sarah Lambert, 177–90. Cardiff: University of Wales Press, 2001.

———. *The New Crusaders: Images of the Crusades in the 19th and Early 20th Centuries*. Aldershot: Ashgate, 2000.

Skottki, Kristin. "The Dead, the Revived and the Recreated Pasts: 'Structural Amnesia' in Representations of Crusade History." In *Perceptions of the Crusades from the Nineteenth to the Twenty-First Century: Engaging the Crusades, Volume One*, edited by Mike Horswell and Jonathan Phillips, 107–33. Abingdon: Routledge, 2018.

Spencer, Stephen J. "'Like a Raging Lion': Richard the Lionheart's Anger During the Third Crusade in Medieval and Modern Historiography." *English Historical Review* 556 (2017): 495–532.

Taylor, Nicholas, and Gerald Vorhees. "Introduction: Masculinity and Gaming: Mediated Masculinities in Play." In *Masculinities in Play*, edited by Nicholas Taylor and Gerald Vorhees, 1–19. Cham: Palgrave Macmillan, 2018.

"The More You Know." www.reddit.com/r/insanepeoplefacebook/comments/bgqwsb/the_more_you_know/. Accessed August 18, 2020.

Trammell, Aaron. "Militarism and Masculinity in *Dungeons & Dragons*." In *Masculinities in Play*, edited by Nicholas Taylor and Gerald Vorhees, 129–48. Cham: Palgrave Macmillan, 2018.

Walsh, Timothy J., and John T. Sebastian. "Shades of Dante: Virtual Bodies in *Dante's Inferno*." In *Digital Gaming Re-imagines the Middle Ages*, edited by Daniel T. Kline, 162–74. London: Routledge, 2014.

Weisl, Angela Jane, and Kevin J. Stevens. "The Middle Ages in the Depths of Hell: Pedagogical Possibility and the Past in *Dante's Inferno*." In *Digital Gaming Re-imagines the Middle Ages*, edited by Daniel T. Kline, 175–86. London: Routledge, 2014.

# 3 'Show this fool knight what it is to have no fear'

## Freedom and oppression in *Assassin's Creed* (2007)

*Oana-Alexandra Chirilă*

In 2007, Ubisoft launched what was to become the first title in one of the most iconic video game franchises in recent history. Since then, *Assassin's Creed* has spawned over ten other major titles, additional minor ones, more than one book series and a big-budget Hollywood film, not to mention countless instances of fanfiction. There are no signs that the *Assassin's Creed* craze is going to end any time soon.

The main plot line of the series is the unseen power struggle between two factions, the Assassins, modelled after the real-life Ismaili Nizaris, and the Templars, modelled after the Order of the Knights Templar, a war that has been going on throughout human history, behind closed doors and without the general population's knowledge. This fictional ongoing hidden battle has allowed Ubisoft to reenact very diverse time periods, such as the Italian Renaissance (*Assassin's Creed II*, *Assassin's Creed Brotherhood*), the American Revolution (*Assassin's Creed III*), or the French Revolution (*Assassin's Creed Unity*), while the latest instalment, *Assassin's Creed Odyssey* (2018), takes the player on a journey based in Pericles' Athens. Our focus, however, falls on the first title of the franchise, *Assassin's Creed*, which is set during the Third Crusade (1189–1192). The game received multiple awards and by 2009 it had already sold over eight million copies.[1]

In the *Assassin's Creed* universe, both the Assassins and the Templars are searching for the Pieces of Eden, ancient mysterious objects that possess supernatural powers. At a first glance, the Assassins want to use these objects to liberate mankind by giving the people access to knowledge while the Templars are presented as oppressors who desire to use the Pieces of Eden to keep the population under control. The player's introduction into this world is made through Desmond Miles, a present-day bartender and descendant from a long line of Assassins who has been kidnapped by the Abstergo Corporation. This corporation, which is in fact run by the Templars, has developed a peculiar machine called the Animus that allows the subject to relive their ancestors' memories, all in order to locate a certain Piece of Eden. When Desmond is connected to the Animus, he becomes able to access the memories of Altaïr Ibn-La'Ahad, an Assassin from the Third Crusade who is believed to have seen that particular object. Altaïr's story begins with him as a Master Assassin in Syria's Masyaf. After failing a mission given by his leader, Al-Mualim, Altaïr is stripped of his rank and forced to rework his way up from novice to Master. In order to do this, he is given a list of nine assassination targets whom he can find in the cities of Acre, Jerusalem, and Damascus. While the game occasionally switches back and forth between the two stories, the majority of the gameplay focuses on Altaïr and his task, thus making him the true protagonist of the instalment.

It is evident that *Assassin's Creed* does not present itself as a true-to-form reconstitution of the past. From the very beginning, the producers let us know that it is a 'work of fiction'. To quote creative director Patrice Desilets, 'this is not a historical game. It is a Sci-Fi universe in which you play in a historical setting'.[2] In her article 'The Dead, the Revived and the Recreated Pasts. Structural Amnesia in Representations of Crusade History', scholar Kristin Skottki argues that when we speak of the past we actually speak of three different pasts: 'the dead past encapsulated in the historical source material; the revived pasts of memories, imagination and reenactments of historical events that still (or again) surround us today; and the recreated pasts of historical reconstructions'.[3] However, they all require a 'present', which is both the contemporaneity and the subjective lens through which an individual either revives the past, looks at the revived pasts, or recreates the past.

My goal is to demonstrate that by employing both instances of revived pasts as well as of recreated pasts, or what we can call the academic endeavour to search for the historical truth, as well as by playing on the subject of memory, *Assassin's Creed* in fact hides a deeper concern very relevant to the modern world: the opposition between freedom and oppression of thought. Lars Konzack suggests that 'video games are able to present worlds and ideas to us in a new way',[4] through what he calls 'philosophical game design'. Moreover, 'even if a game designer does not intentionally control and design the philosophy behind the game, one will exist anyway'.[5] If the developer does have a world picture that they want to incorporate in the game, they need 'to know the history of ideas, and how to present metaphysical ideas, turning them into consistent game constructions through the creative processes'.[6] This chapter, therefore, looks at the means through which the developers were able to mitigate different perceptions of the Nizaris and the philosophy of the game. In doing so, we must ask ourselves:

how does *Assassin's Creed* position itself in relation to discourses on the crusades, specifically those on the Nizaris? And more importantly, what can *Assassin's Creed* teach us about how we look at, or should look at, history?

Traditional perspectives on the long-spanning series of conflicts that we usually call the 'crusades' see them from a deeply Eurocentric point of view and in an oversimplified manner: Christianity versus Islam, where Muslims are the oppressors. The validity of the crusaders' cause is never questioned and the Arab perspective is never taken into consideration. In this paradigm, not only are Islam and the Arab world seen as a monolithic, homogenous block, but everything about them will be seen as inherently different, and thus qualitatively inferior to their Christian/ European counterpart, a paradigm of thought that Edward Said called 'orientalism'. According to Said, orientalism 'is a style of thought based upon an ontological and epistemological distinction made between "the Orient" and "the Occident" '.[7] Moreover, Said sees orientalism as a Western invention dedicated to the domination of the Orient.[8] Therefore, Western depictions of the Orient can be seen to make a clear distinction between the civilised Occident and the barbaric Orient, which the now infamous term 'clash of civilizations' coined by Bernard Lewis attempts to prove can never be reconciled. Such a simplistic worldview minimises if not entirely forgets the complexity of historical reality.[9]

*Assassin's Creed* plays with this interpretation of history. First, it switches the focus from the crusader's journey to that of the inhabitant of the Levant. Second, while at a first glance there seems to appear a clear dichotomy between the Assassins and the Templars, where the former should be the heroes and the latter the villains, the more the story unfolds the more Altaïr, and through him Desmond and ultimately the player, learns that the world is not black and white. Third, the crusades in themselves have no meaning. Their spatiality and temporality are used only as a background for the story and they tell us nothing about the characters' inner qualities. As Frank Bosman puts it, '*Assassin's Creed* refuses to use the stereotyped division between good guys and bad guys based on ethnical or religious divisions'.[10] Not coincidentally, in their works, the two historians that helped during the game's development, David Nicolle[11] and Paul Cobb,[12] both strongly advocate against the 'clash of civilizations' narrative by emphasising the intricate social and political realities of twelfth-century Levant. *Assassin's Creed* starts from the premise that the player is somewhat familiar with the historical setting of the game. Moreover, it assumes that they are at least in some measure captive to stereotypes about the crusades and to those proposed by the 'clash of civilizations'. It then goes on to deconstruct these stereotypes and present a fresh view both of the past and the present.

The game does this through a twofold dialogue: the dialogue between Altaïr and his environment and the one between him and Desmond.

## The Ismaili Nizaris and the Assassins

Altaïr is first and foremost an Assassin in the Levant. This is his only identity marker. We do not know anything about his origins or upbringing because they are of no relevance to the game or story. He is an Assassin through and through. But who are the Assassins? While obviously modelled after the Nizaris, a clear distinction should be made between the real-life Nizaris (the dead past), the legends that surround them (revived pasts), and the in-game order of the Assassins (revived pasts + recreated pasts). Much of what we know about the sect comes from external sources, mainly from relatively contemporary Muslim scholars who were at odds with the Nizaris[13] or from later European authors who kept embellishing on already established stories to fit their own agenda. Therefore, we should keep in mind that our access to the Nizaris is 'volatile, fractious, and mediated'.[14]

The Nizaris, a branch of the Shia Ismailis, were founded by Hassan ibn Sabbah in 1094 after the Fatimid caliph Al-Mustansir's death. While most believed that his son Musta'il should be the successor, ibn Sabbah considered Al-Mustansir's other son, Nizar, as the caliph's rightful heir to the Imamate. Before this, Hassan had been a faithful ally of Al-Mustansir's in Iran, conquering various fortresses in the caliph's name. The most famous of them would be Alamut (1090), eventually the Nizaris' headquarters. Apart from their distinctive religious belief, two of their characteristics were reclusiveness and the conduct of marked killings. In order to survive and thrive and knowing that they would be outnumbered in a full-on war against the other factions in the area, Hassan's people resorted to killing specific key persons, more often than not sacrificing themselves in the process. Over time, the general public began associating them with a far larger number of murders than they had actually undertaken. In reality, the Nizaris were more prone to strike diplomatic deals, having done so with the Order of the Knights Templar,[15] the sultan Salah ad-Din,[16] and even the Mongols.[17] While a minority among the Shia, the Nizaris exist to this day, numbering several millions and speaking a multitude of languages.[18]

Their image in the West, and elsewhere, is, however, a considerably more fantastical one. It is one that was built over centuries and it has to do more with the stuff of legends. The Nizaris' peculiarities and reclusiveness fascinated diverse authors who, in order to convey their own messages, filled in the gaps with stories of whose veracity is questionable at best. *Assassin's Creed* makes use of these stories not in order to give them validity but, on the contrary, to emphasise both its own and their surrealness. For the purpose of this chapter I will identify the following: the legend of the Garden of Paradise, the meaning of *hashishiyya*, the legend of the 'leap of faith', and the belief regarding their creed.

According to the *Qur'an*, the Garden of Paradise is filled with colourful flowers, rivers of abundance, and beautiful maidens that await the believer.[19] In order to gain his acolytes' complete obedience and trust, the story says that Hassan used to drug his soldiers with a mysterious plant before taking them to a simulacrum of this garden. This, coupled with the fact that contemporary outsiders used to call the Nizaris *hashishiyya*, led Silvestre de Sacy to link the derogatory term with hashish. According to de Sacy, *hashishiyya* means 'those who consume hashish'.[20] No etymology has been universally accepted around this term and there is no compelling evidence that the Nizaris actually used to use hashish. Another proposed meaning of the term would be that it is a corrupted version of the word *hassas*, which is used widely by Syrians and Egyptians to describe a thief or someone with evil intentions.[21] It is worth stressing the fact that the Nizaris never called themselves *hashishiyya*. However, not only did the name stick, but it is also the origin of the English word 'Assassin'. While it had been made popular in the West first by travellers such as Friar Odoric[22] and Marco Polo,[23] this story was also the main plot point in Vladimir Bartol's highly successful novel *Alamut* (1938).

Even though the game prominently makes use of the term *Assassin*, its proposed etymology and its connection to the legend of the Garden are not so obviously integrated. As a matter of fact, one would have to know the stories beforehand to even notice any hint pointing at them. If one walks freely in the citadel, the player can enter a garden populated by women dressed in 'harem-style' clothing, such as shalwars, and adorned with gold jewellery. Unless the player chooses to roam around and enter this garden, no other sign of it exists throughout the game. Moreover, when Al-Mualim strips Altaïr of his rank, the leader stabs him, but the next day Altaïr wakes up miraculously unwounded. This could be interpreted as a hint that he had actually been drugged, an observation that Bosman also makes.[24] Another instance in the franchise that might be linked to the hashish legend can be found in *Assassin's Creed: Unity* when Arno, the protagonist, drinks from a potion during the initiation ritual, gaining access to what seems to be a higher level of consciousness. The name of the potion or its ingredients are never mentioned. Both the stabbing episode and the ritualistic potion serve only to add to the surrealness of the game's story and as plot devices.

As far as the legend of the 'leap of faith' is concerned, the first author to mention it was Arnold von Lübeck,[25] who states that when Henry II of Champagne arrived at Masyaf in 1194 for a meeting with Sinan Al-Rashid, the Syrian Nizaris' leader at that time, Sinan ordered some of his followers to throw themselves off the citadel's walls, presumably committing suicide. According to von Lübeck, this feature impressed the invader so much that he eventually left the Nizaris unharmed.[26] Modern research, however, has suggested that these were staged,[27] a detail that becomes of crucial importance in the game. In *Assassin's Creed*, whenever Altaïr needs to come down off a building fast, he can perform a 'leap of faith' by throwing himself (in especially marked places) into a haystack. This feature is used far and wide as to save the player time and to make the game more enticing. Our introduction to the leap of faith is made in the beginning of the game during a character named Robert de Sablè's attack on Masyaf. When de Sablè arrives at the gates of the citadel, Al-Mualim orders three of his followers, Altaïr among them, to throw themselves off the citadel's walls and into the steep valley that surrounds it, by saying 'Show this fool knight what it is to have no fear', the quote that also gives our chapter its title. Once again, the use of the leap of faith in the game is not done in order to reaffirm the legend, but because it makes sense within the universe, it blends with the game's mechanics and it gives the player a thrilling experience, as the heights are, more often than not, impressive.

Other commonly believed myths about the Nizaris that have been to some extent incorporated into the game are that of the cutting of the ring finger to accommodate the hidden dagger and that of their clothing. While it might be true that the Nizaris used to use daggers as assassination weapons,[28] which required them to gain close proximity to the target, there is no evidence that they had had their fingers removed.[29] In the game, the dagger becomes both a plot point and a convenient way to switch between styles of play, combat and stealth, in order to suit any kind of player. The gauntlet and the hidden blade that is attached to it are now an iconic image of the game. As far as their clothing is concerned, Joseph von Hammer (1818) says that their robes were white, a statement also made by Gustav Flügel,[30] but their bonnets, boots, and belts used to be red, therefore using similar colours as the Templars. Hammer also observes their alleged sartorial choices resembled that of the Sufis, but that the Master's robe was also white.[31] This is in contradiction to Sufi orders such as the Mevlevi; during the *sema* the dervishes relinquish their black capes, but the *murshid* keeps his on as a sign of hierarchical status. Interestingly, in the game, low-rank Assassins wear white robes (with red embellishments) and high-rank ones wear black robes, especially Al-Mualim, whose garments are black and gold.

## Nothing is true, everything is permitted

A main focus point of the game, however, is the creed of the Assassin's, 'Nothing is true, everything is permitted'. The game's name is, after all, *Assassin's Creed*. The phrase is not an invention of the producers, but it has been linked to the Nizaris for centuries. In 1867, Flügel mentions that the Nizaris' motto was *Nichtz zu glauben und Alles thun zu dürfen*,[32] which can be translated to 'Not to believe anything and be allowed to do anything'. He also states that this revelation was only meant for those of the highest ranks. Later, while praising the Nizaris for their supposed freedom of thought, Friedrich Nietzsche repeats this information.[33] Building on this, the so-called creed of the Assassins becomes a central point in Bartol's novel *Alamut*.[34] It comes as no surprise that the game developers used Bartol's book as a source of inspiration for the game, Raymond admitting it openly.[35] However, there is no evidence to suggest such a creed ever existed.

In reality, the creed seems to be a summary of the *qiyamah*, 'Resurrection', that is believed to have been proclaimed by Imam Hassan at Alamut in 1164. Eventually, although not readily, the Syrian Nizaris also accepted the reformation.[36] While Shia Islam, and particularly Ismailism, had always had a more esoteric component than its Sunni counterpart, Hassan's *qiyamah* emphasised the importance of the *batin*, 'the hidden', in contrast to the *zahir*, 'the apparent'. Hermetic in nature, the *batin/zahir* has traditionally been applied in Shia Islam to the reading of the *Qur'an*. Hassan's understanding of the dichotomy, however, moves forward and, coupled with the idea of cyclical time, translates it to the Imam. He names himself as the Revealed Imam, a 'reincarnation' of the Imam archetype that started with Adam.[37] His figure becomes of the utmost importance for the Nizaris, that of a sun around which planets orbit. According to Henry Corbin, 'what the proclamation implied was nothing less than the coming of a pure spiritual Islam, freed from all spirit of legalism and of all enslavement to the Law'.[38] While there is no substantial evidence of the Nizaris' rejection of the *Shari'a* after the reformation, it is easy to understand why non-initiates such as the European travellers and thinkers might have confused their esotericism with hedonistic freedom.

In the game, the creed becomes 'a radical, phenomenological approach to reality: all human knowledge is relative and contextual'.[39] The *batin/zahir* dichotomy in the game's philosophy can be interpreted on a multitude of levels of understanding. For Altaïr, it gradually becomes clear that his beliefs, his most sacred convictions that he had been holding as absolute truths, are anything but that and this forces him to reconsider both his environment as well as, consequently, his position in it. Desmond witnesses these events from the point of view of his own metal constructions and he, in turn, is forced to recalibrate his place in the world. Finally, it is the player's turn to acknowledge the relativity and subjectivity of his experience. Like Desilets observes, 'there is no dogma, only the one you accept'.[40] Moving the *Assassin's Creed* story from one historical setting to another does nothing else than to universalise the creed as part of the human philosophical experience.

## Altaïr Ibn-La'ahad and Al-Mualim

While 'Nothing is true, everything is permitted' promotes freedom of thought, the concept can only be understood in contrast to a restriction of thought. While we would be inclined to think that these ideas' embodiments are the Assassins on one hand and the Templars on the other, this is true only on a superficial level. The opposition becomes clearer when looked at through the antithesis between Altaïr and his Master, Al-Mualim. In the beginning of the game, Altaïr, although arrogant in his actions, never questions Al-Mualim's intentions and orders. Whatever Al-Mualim asks of him, Altaïr does. As the story progresses, with every assassination, Altaïr learns something new about his environment and starts questioning both himself and his master's actions. In the end, the final battle Altaïr has to engage in is not with a Templar, as he had previously thought it would be, but with Al-Mualim. As the protagonist, and thus the player through him, comes to learn, the person that had been keeping the three cities in chaos was Al-Mualim himself, as he wanted the Piece of Eden for his personal gain, not for the liberation of mankind. By killing Al-Mualim and taking his place as the leader of the Assassins, Altaïr defeated his inner demons and prejudices and is now in pure control of his mind and actions.

Signs foreshadowing this final battle do exist throughout the game. First, on the exterior, their garments are in perfect opposition, as Altaïr's robe is white and Al-Mualim's is black. While this is a sign of Al-Mualim's high-rank within the order, it is also one of his dark nature. Al-Mualim is blind of one eye, more specifically his right eye, a characteristic that, with the exception of a few scenes, is barely visible. This blindness in one eye can be interpreted in a number of ways. First, it can be a reflection of his old age. Second, players familiar with Norse mythology might link it with the god Odin who sacrificed one of his eyes for knowledge,[41] an interpretation that, on the level of his searching for the Piece of Eden, fits the character very well. However, according to the Islamic faith, in the Last Days, Masih Al-Dajjal will appear, a figure comparable to the Christian Antichrist. As stated by the *ahadith*, he will be blind of his right eye and his purpose will be to subdue the entire world to his will.⁴² The right eye in a man is dedicated to contemplating spiritual things and the left one to look at the material. Being blind in the right eye is a symbol of Al-Dajjal's lack of interest for the spiritual and proneness for the material,⁴³ a characteristic of Al-Mualim's that Altaïr, and the player through him, eventually comes to learn. It is also no coincidence that he is searching for an object called 'Piece of Eden', this being an obvious reference to the biblical Tree of Knowledge, another story about free will. Moreover, it resembles a royal orb, a monarch's sign of power and a symbol of eventual world domination.⁴⁴ As far as his name is concerned, Al-Mualim literally means 'the teacher', and therefore he does not have a name of his own. Even though, in later Nizari writings, the leader is called *al-mu'allim*, and even though associations between in-game Al-Mualim and real Nizari historical figures such as Hassan ibn Sabbah or Sinan Ar-Rashid can be made, the Assassin is neither of them, but a metonymy for all that teaches one what to think and how to act.

In opposition lies Altaïr. In the beginning of the game he is an arrogant Master Assassin, who got to his position by blindly following Al-Mualim's orders and who thinks he knows everything there is to know about the world. After a fatal mistake, he is stripped of his rank and has to once more climb the hierarchical ladder. While this is a perfect pretext for the player to gain experience within the game, it is also symbolic of the fact we are witnessing a turning point in Altaïr's life. Whatever he did before the beginning of the game does not interest us because it was done without free will or critical thinking, but merely at Al-Mualim's orders. Altaïr is only now embarking on a quest of self-discovery and self-liberation. Not at all coincidentally, his symbol is the eagle. Outside of the game's philosophy, it is true that Alamut, the Nizaris' headquarters in Iran, can be translated as 'the eagle's nest'. Inside, however, Altaïr's symbolic animal is one that flies free of all constraints, much as the Assassin learns to do. The eagle motif can be seen throughout the game, starting with Altaïr's name, an abbreviation of the Arabic *an-nasr at-ta'ir*, 'the flying eagle'. It is also the name of the brightest star in the eagle constellation and, serendipitously, the name of the first personal computer. Altaïr's robe's back is designed to resemble the tail of an eagle and the hood its peak. Whenever he performs a 'leap of faith', an eagle sound can be heard and his shadow looks like one of an eagle's. In addition, he has an 'eagle-vision' skill which can be used to scrutinise the environment. On the other hand, the eagle is a bird of prey, one that kills in order to survive, a fact also relevant and revealing for Altaïr's story. His last name, however, ibn-La'Ahad, means 'son of none', once again suggesting the fact that his story before the starting of the game is not important. It is also a sign of his struggle for liberation and, as Al-Mualim's name stands for those who inject thoughts in others, Altaïr's is a metonymy for those that reject preformed ideas and thoughts.

This is also evident by the fact that Altaïr's face is always covered, thus allowing the player to project whatever facial features they wish. To quote Connie Veugen, this gives the player 'a blank canvas' which makes it easier to identify with the character.[45] Initially, Altaïr was supposed to have a Middle Eastern accent,[46] but in the final product his speech is entirely American. According to the game's producer, Jade Raymond, the reason for Altaïr's American accent is that it is not really Altaïr speaking, but Desmond through the Animus.[47] Therefore, we are once again confronted with the issue of free will. The player controls Desmond, who is being held captive by Abstergo, but who controls Altaïr who is also being controlled by Al-Mualim. While it may seem that the player is the one above the chess board, this is not true, since they are also forced to submit to the limits of the game's mechanics and story. However, since the game falls into the category of 'sandbox' games, in which the player can choose what quests and in which order to do them, and since one can either run through it in combat mode or take their time using stealth, the player 'is given the freedom to experience this adventure in a manner that fits their individual play style'.[48] Thus, the theme of freedom versus oppression can be applied to the game itself.[49]

## The environment

Apart from the *qiyamah*, another concept that is important in the context of the Nizaris is *taqiyya*, the art of dissimulation. In order to gain proximity to his target, the Nizari soldier acted like a spy, blending first into the society and then making his move. This concept has been marvellously adapted into the game, giving the player the possibility to make use of the stealth mode. Through features such as blending, eavesdropping, and pickpocketing, the player can access restricted areas by infiltrating groups of scholars on the go, listen to private conversations, and gather classified information. Other data-gathering tools are informants and the Assassins Bureau, small offices of the order that can be found in every city. Moreover, the game takes place on two separate levels, the street level and the rooftop level, and each requires a different strategy. On the street level, the player needs to be more careful not to get recognised by the guardian soldiers or Templars nor to create a ruckus when in a hurry. The non-player characters (NPCs) that fill the cities are designed to signal whenever Altaïr does something out of the ordinary, such as bumping into jug-carrying women. On the rooftop level, however, the player has a larger freedom to act, since fewer NPCs occupy this space. It is also designed in such a way that Altaïr's parkour-style movements are practically uninhibited, the player being able to make use of different decorations to aid their free-running. Different objects, like haystacks, benches, and rooftop gardens, can be used to hide from alerted soldiers.

Geographically, the environment in which Altaïr moves consists of Masyaf, the Assassins' headquarters, the cities of Jerusalem, Damascus, and Acre, and a middle ground that connects them called 'The Kingdom'. Masyaf, factually the Nizaris' main stronghold at that time, is also divided into two parts: the village, at the bottom of the mountain, and the citadel, on the top of the mountain. While the village is occupied both by non-initiates as well as initiates, recognisable by their similar clothing to Altaïr's, the citadel is home only to the Assassins. More importantly, it is also where Al-Mualim's office is. His personal space, situated on the top floor of the citadel, is filled with books, scrolls, and incense burners. The lights are dim and the atmosphere is sort of magical, denoting the leader's vast knowledge in both the exoteric as well as the esoteric. Whenever Altaïr needs to meet with his master, the player cannot escape climbing the mountain and the stairs that eventually lead to Al-Mualim's office. Symbolically, this journey represents Altaïr's personal quest for knowledge, wisdom, and understanding that he believes only Al-Mualim can give him. Al-Mualim never leaves this office and his only connections with the outside world are either through his followers or through carrier pigeons, a detail of no little importance. Such as the carrier pigeons are messengers that always find their way back to him, so are the Assassins whom he had trained in perfect obedience.

As far as the three main cities go, while highly similar, each has a particular design style. Regular buildings such as houses maintain a Middle Eastern architecture. They are close to the street, have hidden gardens, and the windows are covered in order to maintain the privacy of their inhabitants. The streets are both narrow and wide, depending on the area, and one can also find different fountains or urban decorations. Important landmarks in each city have been kept, such as the Grand Mosque in Damascus, and they have been rendered with very high accuracy in rapport to the originals. From these, Altaïr can synchronise with the environment by using his eagle-vision and perform leaps of faith on his way down. The cities' skylines are grazed by colourful minarets embellished in Arabic calligraphy. However, they are cylindrical in shape, not square as they actually are in the Levant and the calligraphy is one that is, in reality, generally used in the Maghreb.[50] Nevertheless, these minor inconsistencies do not steal from the immersive experience since the general public are unlikely to be aware of them.

The population that fills these cities is heterogeneous, people having different types of clothing and different complexions. Sometimes these details betray a possible cultural background for the respective NPC. For instance, women with a darker complexion tend to have their heads covered, suggesting a Muslim background, while lighter-skinned ones flaunt their locks, suggesting a Christian (European) one. A multitude of preachers give *ad-hoc* lectures in public spaces and merchants invite passers-by to take a look at their goods. These include spices, leather clothing, and colourful pottery. All of these are consistent with how the atmosphere in a Levantine city should have been at the time of the Third Crusade. Due to technical limitations, children and animals are missing.[51] Acre has a bleaker atmosphere than Jerusalem and Damascus, reflecting the bloody siege the city had just gone through. The colours are more green-hued, suggesting disease, and countless decaying corpses can be seen on the streets. Black smoke covers the air and a large number of buildings are rendered to look like ruins. The population is also generally poorer than in the other cities, Altaïr being continuously harassed by beggars and drunkards. Last but not least, 'The Kingdom' acts as a middle passage between the four main regions. While going through it, the player can choose to walk, run, or ride horseback, a choice that saves time. This middle passage is not a wasteland, but a vibrant place where Altaïr can have more adventures: towers from which he can synchronise, soldiers to avoid or defeat in combat, flags to gather, and so on. Small villages populated by civilians can also be found.

While the gameplay can, at times, feel repetitive, roaming the virtual streets of twelfth century Levantine cities is a delight. As Raymond confirms, a lot of work has been put into exactly this:

> We contacted a historian early in the conception phase of development to help us build a foundation of research. We have used the web, documentaries, old medieval encyclopaedias, paintings, and novels. The historian helped us with some harder to find information such as original city plans of Jerusalem, Damascus, and Acre that date back to the Third Crusade.[52]

Over time, bigger budgets and better technology have allowed the creators to recreate fantastically close-to-the-original virtual models of famous buildings. According to the media, research used in creating the 3D model of the Notre-Dame in *Assassin's Creed: Unity* will be used in the reconstruction of the real Notre-Dame cathedral in the aftermath of the April 2019 fire.[53]

## Discussion

In the months following the tragic events of 11 September 2001, 'there was a strong concentration of media references to the Assassins legends',[54] tying the Nizaris to terrorism and trying to promote a fabricated millennium-old inclination of Muslims towards violence. Not only that, but Bernard Lewis' seminal 1967 book *The Assassins. A Radical Sect in Islam*, whose cover uses the word 'terror' in both its English and French versions, was quickly republished (2002) by Basic Books in a fresh new edition. Obviously, 'links were made between the Assassins and the Al-Qaeda's attacks'.[55] The 'clash of civilizations' was once again being used in public discourse. When *Assassin's Creed* launched, the whole Western world, and especially the United States, was still involved in the 'War on Terror'. So, as Veugen puts it, 'from a historical and cultural point of view the launch of this game at that particular moment in time is, to say the least, interesting'.[56] It is meant to be interpreted through twenty-first-century eyes. In this context, the game did something unexpected: it turned the so-called Assassins into the good guys. Beforehand, representations of Middle Eastern characters in video games had been scarce, one-dimensional, and almost always tied to violence. First-person shooters usually set their stories in now war-torn countries like Iraq or Afghanistan, and the locals were invariably terrorists who needed to be put down. Not even Ubisoft's previous successful franchise set in the Middle East, *Prince of Persia*, of which *Assassin's Creed* was initially supposed to be a part, managed to change the audience's pre-set ideas of the 'Orient', with its obvious inspiration from *Arabian Nights* stereotypes. But *Assassin's Creed* gave different demographics a new lens through which to view the world: Middle Eastern players now had a mainstream video game culture hero to relate to and Western players were forced to re-evaluate their images of 'the Arab', search for deeper historic truth, and recalibrate their thoughts. The fandom continues to grow exponentially and the material culture that surrounds the game along with it. Starting from 2007, there is no comic-con that doesn't see at least one Altaïr or Ezio cosplayer, no social media platform that doesn't have an *Assassin's Creed* community, and no online marketplace that doesn't sell merchandise tied to the game.

*Assassin's Creed* does not take itself as a recreated past, that is an accurate depiction of the past, but as a vessel for how we interpret both the past and the present. From the very beginning the creators let the player know that the game is 'a work of fiction'. To convey its message, the game blends academic research with established legends not to reinforce the latter, but to put them under a new light. Therefore, whether intentionally or not, *Assassin's Creed* also manages to raise questions regarding the veracity of the ways we deal with and understand the past. The so-called creed, 'Nothing is true, everything is permitted', can be applied to how we perceive history itself, we are unable to reconstruct the past in its entirety, but merely an illusion of it. Every now and then glitches appear on the screen, forcing the player to remember that what they are experiencing is not the truth, but merely a rendition of it. The past is the past and what we can see is only a reconstruction inevitably made and projected from the present. Memories, both personal and collective, are subjective and volatile. Although the Assassins are modelled after the Nizaris, they are not the Nizaris and the Nizaris are not the Assassins. Characters in the game do not act in a certain way because of their ethnic or religious background, but because of their free will and personal desires. This is something that the player comes to learn alongside Altaïr. It is our stereotypes that limit our understanding on the world by fixating our place in it and inhibiting our intentionality. In the beginning of the game, Altaïr has a binary worldview, where the Assassins are good and the Templars are evil, and this, for him, is an absolute age-old truth. Target by target and as the story progresses, Altaïr comes to the realisation that good and evil exist on both sides equally, independent of one's cultural background. Gradually, his understanding of morality changes as he liberates his mind of all those pre-set doctrinal ideas. 'Show this fool knight what it is to have no fear' does not refer to a lack of fear in the face of death, but in the face of life, as truth sets the individual free. That is why, in the end, it was not Robert de Sablè the final enemy Altaïr had to encounter, but himself.

## Notes

1 Huaxin Wei, *Analyzing the Game Narrative: Structure and Technique* (Dissertation, Simon Fraser University, 2011), 103.
2 Richard Moss, "Assassin's Creed: An Oral History," *Polygon*, October 3, 2018, www.polygon.com/features/2018/10/3/17924770/assassins-creed-an-oral-history-patrice-desilets, accessed December 27, 2019.
3 Kristin Skottki, "The Dead, the Revived and the Recreated Pasts: Structural Amnesia in Representations of Crusade History," in *Perceptions of the Crusades from the Nineteenth to the Twenty-First Century*, ed. Mike Horswell and Jonathan Phillips (London: Routledge, 2018), 110.
4 Lars Konzack, "Philosophical Game Design," in *The Video Game Theory Reader 2*, ed. Bernard Perron and Mark J. P. Wolf (New York, NY and London: Routledge, 2009), 33.
5 Ibid., 34.
6 Ibid.
7 Edward Said, *Orientalism* (London: Penguin Books, 2003), 2.
8 Ibid.
9 David Nicolle, *The Crusades* (Chicago, IL: Osprey, 2001), 7.
10 Ibid., 23.
11 See, for instance, David Nicolle, *The Third Crusade 1191: Richard the Lionheart, Saladin and the Struggle for Jerusalem* (Oxford: Osprey, 2006), 7.
12 See, for instance, Paul Cobb, *The Race for Paradise: An Islamic History of the Crusades* (Oxford and New York, NY: Oxford University Press, 2014), 278.
13 Geraldine Heng, "Sex, Lies, and Paradise: The Assassins, Prester John, and the Fabulation of Civilizational Identities," *Differences* 23 (2012): 7.

14 Ibid.
15 Farhad Daftary, *Ismaili Literature: A Bibliography of Sources and Studies* (London: I. B. Tauris, 2004), 369.
16 Ibid., 370.
17 Timothy May, "A Mongol-Isma'ili Alliance? Thoughts on the Mongols and Assassins," *Journal of the Royal Asiatic Society* 3, no. 14 (2004): 231–39.
18 Daftary, *Ismaili Literature*, 1.
19 See, for instance, X:9–10, XVIII:31.
20 David Guba, "Antoine Isaac Silvestre de Sacy and the Myth of the Hachichins: Orientalizing Hashish in Nineteenth-Century France," *Social History of Alcohol and Drugs* 30 (2016): 51.
21 Ibid., 52.
22 James Waterson, *The Ismaili Assassins: A History of Medieval Murder* (London: Frontline Books, 2007), 211.
23 Marco Polo, *The Travels of*, chapter 23.
24 Frank Bosman, "Nothing is True, Everything is Permitted: The Portrayal of the Nizari Isma'ilis in the Assassin's Creed game series," *Heidelberg Journal of Religions on the Internet* 10 (2016): 17.
25 Farhad Daftary, *The Assassin Legends: Myths of the Isma'ilis* (London: I. B. Tauris, 1994), 104.
26 Bosman, "Nothing is True, Everything is Permitted," 16.
27 Ibid., 17.
28 Waterson, *The Ismaili Assassins*, 66.
29 Bosman, "Nothing is True, Everything is Permitted," 17.
30 Gustav Flügel, *Geschichte der Araber* (Leipzig: Webel Verlagshandlung, 1867), 299.
31 Joseph von Hammer, *Ordinul Asasinilor* (Bucharest: Antet, 2001), 48–49.
32 Flügel, *Geschichte der Araber*, 299.
33 Friedrich Nietzsche, *On the Genealogy of Morals: A Polemical Tract* (Arlington, VA: Richer Resources Publications, 2009), 125.
34 This idea is repeated frequently throughout the book. See, for instance, Vladimir Bartol, *Alamut* (Berkeley, CA: North Atlantic Books, 2007), chapter 15.
35 Mirt Komel, "Orientalism in Assassin's Creed: Self-orientalizing the Assassins from Forerunners of Modern Terrorism into Occidentalized Heroes," *Teorija in Praksa* 51, no. 1 (2014): 83.
36 Marshall G. S. Hodgson, *The Order of Assassins: The Struggle of the Early Nizari Isma'ilis Against the Islamic World* (Chicago, IL: Mouton & Co, 1955), 197.
37 Henry Corbin, *History of Islamic Philosophy* (London and New York, NY: Kegan Paul International, 2001), 95.
38 Ibid.
39 Frank Bosman, "Requiescat in Pace: Initiation and Assassination Rituals in the Assassin's Creed Game Series," *Religions* 9, no. 5 (2018): 31.
40 Moss, "Assassin's Creed: An Oral History."
41 Snorri Sturluson, *The Prose Edda: Tales from Norse Mythology* (Berkeley and Los Angeles, CA: University of California Press, 1966), 42–43.
42 Sahih Muslim, *Hadith no. 324*, www.hadithcollection.com, accessed July 17, 2019.
43 Muhammad Ali, *The Antichrist and Gog and Magog* (Columbus, OH: Ahmadiyya Lahore Inc., 1992), 19–20.

44 Moss, "Assassin's Creed: An Oral History."
45 Connie Veugen, "Altaïr Ibn-La'Ahad: Assassin or All-American Hero," *Instituut Voor Maatschappelijke Verbeelding* 2 (2014): 5.
46 Ibid., 8.
47 Magy Seif Al-Nasr, Maha Al-Saati, Simon Niedenthal, and David Milam, "Assassin's Creed: A Multi-Cultural Read," *Loading . . .* 2, no. 3 (2011): 25, http://journals.sfu.ca/loading/index.php/loading/issue/view/4, accessed July 24, 2019.
48 Patrick Kolan, "Assassin's Creed AU Interview: Patrice Desilets," October 22, 2007, www.ign.com/articles/2007/10/22/assassins-creed-au-interview-patrice-desilets, accessed July 24, 2019.
49 Other games that tinker with this idea are 2K Games' *Bioshock* (2007) and Playdead's *Inside* (2016).
50 Majed S. Balela and Darren Mundy, "Analysing Cultural Heritage and its Representation in Video Games," *Authors & Digital Games Research Association DiGRA Proceedings* 15 (2011): 9.
51 Moss, "Assassin's Creed: An Oral History."
52 Al-Nasr et al., "Assassin's Creed: A Multi-Cultural Read," 14.
53 Ben Gilbert, "As France Rebuilds Notre-Dame Cathedral, The French Studio behind "Assassin's Creed" Is Offering Up Its 'over 5000 Hours' of Research on the 800-year-old Monument," April 18, 2019, www.businessinsider.com/notre-dame-fire-assassins-creed-maxime-durand-ubisoft-interview-2019-4, accessed August 7, 2019.
54 Karim H. Karim, "The Legend of the Assassins in News Coverage of Muslims," in *The Oxford Handbook of Religion and Media*, ed. Diane Winston (New York, NY, 2012), 234.
55 Ibid.
56 Veugen, "Altaïr Ibn-La'Ahad," 2.

# Bibliography

Ali, Muhammad. *The Antichrist and Gog and Magog*. Columbus, OH: Ahmadiyya Lahore Inc., 1992.
Al-Nasr, Magy, Maha Al-Saati, Simon Niedenthal, and David Milam. "Assassin's Creed: A Multi-Cultural Read." *Loading . . . The Journal of the Canadian Game Studies Association* 2, no. 3 (2011). http://journals.sfu.ca/loading/index.php/loading/issue/view/4. Accessed July 24, 2019.
Balela, Majed S., and Mundy Darren. "Analysing Cultural Heritage and its Representation in Video Games." *Digital Games Research Association DiGRA Proceedings* 15 (2011): 1–16.
Bartol, Vladimir. *Alamut*. Berkeley, CA: North Atlantic Books, 2007.
Bosman, Frank. "Nothing is True, Everything is Permitted: The Portrayal of the Nizari Isma'ilis in the Assassin's Creed Game Series." *Heidelberg Journal of Religions on the Internet* 10 (2016): 6–26.
———. "Requiescat in Pace: Initiation and Assassination Rituals in the Assassin's Creed Game Series." *Religions* 9, no. 5 (2018): 167–86.
Cobb, Paul. *The Race for Paradise: An Islamic History of the Crusades*. Oxford and New York, NY: Oxford University Press, 2014.

Corbin, Henry. *History of Islamic Philosophy*. London and New York, NY: Kegan Paul International, 2001.

Daftary, Farhad. *Ismaili Literature: A Bibliography of Sources and Studies*. London: I. B. Tauris, 2004.

———. *The Assassin Legends: Myths of the Isma'ilis*. London: I. B. Tauris, 1994.

Flügel, Gustav. *Geschichte der Araber*. Leipzig: Webel Verlagshandlung, 1867.

Gilbert, Ben. "As France Rebuilds Notre-Dame Cathedral, The French Studio behind 'Assassin's Creed' is Offering Up its 'over 5000 Hours' of Research on the 800-year-old Monument," April 18, 2019. www.businessinsider.com/notre-dame-fire-assassins-creed-maxime-durand-ubisoft-interview-2019-4. Accessed August 7, 2019.

Guba, David. "Antoine Isaac Silvestre de Sacy and the Myth of the Hachichins: Orientalizing Hashish in Nineteenth-Century France." *Social History of Alcohol and Drugs* 30 (2016): 50–74.

Heng, Geraldine. "Sex, Lies, and Paradise: The Assassins, Prester John, and the Fabulation of Civilizational Identities." *Differences* 23 (2012): 1–31.

Hodgson, Marshall G. S. *The Order of Assassins: The Struggle of the Early Nizari Isma'ilis Against the Islamic World*. Chicago, IL: Mouton & Co., 1955.

Karim, Karim H. "The Legend of the Assassins in News Coverage of Muslims." In *The Oxford Handbook of Religion and Media*, edited by Diane Winston, 229–42. New York, NY: Oxford University Press, 2012.

Kolan, Patrick. "Assassin's Creed AU Interview: Patrice Desilets." October 22, 2007. www.ign.com/articles/2007/10/22/assassins-creed-au-interview-patrice-desilets. Accessed July 24, 2019.

Komel, Mirt. "Orientalism in Assassin's Creed: Self-orientalizing the Assassins from Forerunners of Modern Terrorism into Occidentalized Heroes." *Teorija in Praksa* 51, no. 1 (2014): 72–90.

Konzack, Lars. "Philosophical Game Design." In *The Video Game Theory Reader 2*, edited by Bernard Perron and Mark J. P. Wolf, 33–44. New York, NY and London: Routledge, 2009.

Lewis, Bernard. *The Assassins: A Radical Sect in Islam*. London: Basic Books, 2002.

May, Timothy. "A Mongol-Isma'ili Alliance? Thoughts on the Mongols and Assassins." *Journal of the Royal Asiatic Society* 3, no. 14 (2004): 231–39.

Moss, Richard. "Assassin's Creed: An Oral History." In *Polygon*, October 3, 2018. www.polygon.com/features/2018/10/3/17924770/assassins-creed-an-oral-history-patrice-desilets. Accessed December 27, 2019.

Nicolle, David. *The Crusades*. Chicago, IL: Osprey, 2001.

———. *The Third Crusade 1191: Richard the Lionheart, Saladin and the Struggle for Jerusalem*. Oxford: Osprey, 2006.

Nietzsche, Friedrich. *On the Genealogy of Morals: A Polemical Tract*. Arlington, VA: Richer Resources Publications, 2009.

Polo, Marco. *The Travels of*. New York, NY: Liverlight Publishing, 1953.

Sahih Muslim. *Hadith no. 324*. www.hadithcollection.com. Accessed July 17, 2019.

Said, Edward. *Orientalism*. London: Penguin Books, 2003.

Skottki, Kristin. "The Dead, the Revived and the Recreated Pasts: Structural Amnesia in Representations of Crusade History." In *Perceptions of the Crusades from the Nineteenth to the Twenty-First Century*, edited by Mike Horswell and Jonathan Phillips, 107–32. London: Routledge, 2018.

Sturluson, Snorri. *The Prose Edda: Tales from Norse Mythology*. Berkeley and Los Angeles, CA: University of California Press, 1966.

Van Neunen, Tom. "Touring the Animus: Assassin's Creed and Ludotopical Movement." *Loading . . . The Journal of the Canadian Game Studies Association* 10, no. 17 (2017): 22–39.

Veugen, Connie. "Altaïr Ibn-La'Ahad: Assassin or All-American Hero." *Instituut Voor Maatschappelijke Verbeelding* 2 (2014): 1–12.

———. "Using Games to Mediate History." In *Companion to European Heritage Revivals*, edited by Linde Egberts and Koos Bosma, 95–111. Amsterdam: Springer, 2014.

Von Hammer, Joseph. *Ordinul Asasinilor*. Bucharest: Antet, 2001.

Waterson, James. *The Ismaili Assassins: A History of Medieval Murder*. London: Frontline Books, 2007.

Wei, Huaxin. "Analyzing the Game Narrative: Structure and Technique." Dissertation, Simon Fraser University, Vancouver, 2011.

# 4 Crusader kings too?

## (Mis)Representations of the crusades in strategy games

*Robert Houghton*

Grand Strategy Games – which cast the player as the ruler of a kingdom or other medieval polity – vary substantially in their scope, detail and focus but almost invariably equate 'medieval' with 'crusader'. This may take the form of minor cosmetic features as in the *Civilization* series which do not fundamentally change how the game is played but root its theme within the historical period. There may be more dramatic mechanical elements such as the dedicated crusading system in the *Medieval: Total War* games. Most blatantly, the centrality of the crusades may be suggested through the title of the game as is the case with the *Crusader Kings* series. This privileging of the crusades is perhaps unsurprising as the movement has provided source material for games across all genres, but the tendency may be particularly pronounced amongst Grand Strategy Games. This genre tends to focus on armed struggle as this is comparatively easy to model and is traditionally viewed as the central appeal of the genre.[1] The crusades are one of the most easily and widely identified conflicts of the period and are hence a natural fit for such games set in the Middle Ages.

This focus on the crusades provides substantial potential for a deep consideration of the events which could cement a stronger understanding of the period and challenge the misuse of the crusades in the modern world for political means. But, as tends to be the case with games across genres, Grand Strategy Games typically fall short in their representations of the crusades. In this chapter I will argue that several of the most serious of these shortcomings are the consequence of limitations imposed by design constraints and by the expectations of the genre held by its players and creators.

Grand Strategy Games can be especially influential over their players' understanding of the past.[2] These games are complex and often intricately detailed, presenting the player with quantified data pertaining to their kingdom and those of their computer-controlled opponents,[3] and giving the impression of a thoroughly researched and authoritative source.[4] This detailed data set is required for the construction of the game's mechanics which presents an argument about how the medieval world functioned, allowing the player to engage with these mechanics to develop an understanding of cause and effect.[5] Further, the player must engage with these mechanics and the arguments they represent in order to progress in the game.[6] They must learn the game's version of history.

Although these qualities grant games of the Grand Strategy genre the potential to be powerful teaching tools,[7] they can spread outdated or questionable visions of the past just as effectively. This is an issue as Grand Strategy Games often present problematic or limited visions of history.[8] Beyond the underlying issues present across historical games of all genres, Grand Strategy Games possess additional baggage: they are usually especially Eurocentric;[9] their play tends towards imperialism;[10] they often present history as a pre-ordained chronology of progress towards enlightenment;[11] they tend towards abstraction of complex issues.[12] These games have difficulty representing complex events like the crusades which do not fit easily with the core mechanics of the genre.

Furthermore, Grand Strategy Games (like all games) struggle to portray nuance of arguments and theories. These games rely on absolute quantifiable data as their foundation: when this data can't be found it must be manufactured through educated reasoning.[13] There is no room for debate within the game's databases. Moreover, the mechanics of these games, and hence the arguments they represent, must be portrayed as absolutes for the game to function. For example, the crusades are presented in *Medieval: Total War II* as any war by Catholics against non-Catholics (including heretics and excommunicates) sponsored by the pope. This converges with one modern school of thought which describes the crusades in this very broad geographical scope and strongly centres the role of the pope as the instigator of these expeditions.[14] However, this approach disregards another school which presents the crusades solely as expeditions to the Holy Land,[15] and a third which considers any Catholic holy war to be a crusade regardless of papal support.[16] As Tyerman and Constable have demonstrated, this debate is still very much alive within the academy.[17] However, through this necessarily rigid mechanic, the game promotes one particular definition of the crusades and erases all others.[18]

It should be noted that many of these issues can be resolved through more careful and considered game design. More nuanced objectives and mechanics can encourage play away from the standard model of technological progress.[19] Consideration of history from a global perspective, consultation with representatives of different cultures, and more meaningful mechanical distinctions across historical cultures could provide a more thoughtful and thorough model of the past.[20] Tighter chronological or thematic focus can allow deeper mechanics and an avoidance of oversimplification. Design which supports user-modification or counter-play can allow the debate and rebuttal of the game's mechanics and arguments within and around the game.[21]

But the creators of Grand Strategy Games face several underlying difficulties which emerge from the tension between the complex nature of the crusades, and the design conventions, technological limitations, and player expectations which govern the mechanics and approach of this genre. These issues limit the ability of designers to alter the game's model and hence its representation of the crusades, even though there is a growing demand for a more detailed exploration of these events and several design studios have demonstrated a willingness to devote resources to this end.

In this chapter I will use examples from the *Civilization, Medieval: Total War*, and *Crusader Kings* series of games to highlight three core issues which limit the ability of games of this genre to provide a deep representation of the crusades:

1 The broad and open-ended nature of Grand Strategy Games leads their creators to present oversimplified and arbitrary explanations for the causes of the crusades.
2 The tendency of these games to focus on the highest echelons of political society restricts the ability of their creators to depict the composition of the crusades with sufficient nuance.
3 Traditional structures governing victory conditions and other objectives within this genre of game and the expectations this has built within the playerbase has limited their capacity to consider the goals of the various crusaders.

I will then use *Holy Fury*, the recent expansion for *Crusader Kings II*, as a case study of a recent attempt to develop a more detailed consideration of the crusades and argue that while this is a substantial improvement, it is nevertheless hindered by the conventions of the genre. Throughout the piece I will argue that the creation of a more nuanced representation of the crusades requires a substantial and fundamental change in approach.

## The causes of the crusades

Although the crusades appear widely within Grand Strategy Games, the creators of these games almost universally ignore the causes of the movement. Most representations of the crusades within these games are triggered by arbitrary actions by the player or a computer actor. In *Civilization II* the military unit 'Crusaders' is unlocked through the research of the technology 'Monotheism' while the unique building 'King Richard's Crusade' may be constructed after acquiring knowledge of 'Engineering'. *Medieval: Total War* requires a player or computer actor to construct a series of buildings before creating a 'Crusade' which may then be targeted against a non-Catholic faction. In each of these cases, the crusades are inevitable regardless of the situation within the game.

This is an unsatisfactory approach. The causes of the crusades were complex and remain a subject of academic discourse. They were driven by events over the preceding centuries including the claim to a clerical monopoly on violence through the Peace and Truce of God movements and Church-sponsored military action,[22] the rise of a culture of pilgrimage to Jerusalem,[23] and the centring of the Pope on the international stage through the Investiture Contest.[24] The arbitrary triggers used by *Civilization* and the *Medieval: Total War* games ignore these elements and present the crusades as an inevitable and straightforward conflict.

In principle Grand Strategy Games should be powerful and versatile tools for investigating the causes of the crusades. Presenting cause and effect is one of the greatest strengths of these games in the classroom.[25] By interacting with detailed mechanics, their players consider abstract but holistic explanations of historical systems.[26] By experimenting with different sequences of actions, these players can observe the designers' explanation of the causes of historical events.[27] There is little reason in theory why games of this genre should not be able to provide a deep and developed consideration of the causes of the crusades.

In practice though, the creators of Grand Strategy Games face design and commercial constraints which restrict their ability to address the origins of the crusades in depth. This is primarily because of the discord between three fundamental issues: the open-ended nature of Grand Strategy Games; the resources required to simulate a unique series of events such as the crusades; and audience expectations that the crusades should follow a particular broad pattern within the game.

Grand Strategy Games are the antithesis of linear narrative. Broad victory conditions are assigned, but players receive little guidance in achieving these objectives.[28] Players of these games have a huge amount of agency and a corresponding ability to create unexpected and improbable outcomes. Furthermore, various computer-controlled actors react to player choices and the developing environment with their own goals beyond the player's control. The game world therefore evolves in organised chaos. The possible versions of history produced by these games are effectively limitless and although creators usually attempt to guide this towards a realistic or balanced emergent history, there is little they can do in the face of a determined player or a particularly unlikely set of events. This open-ended gameplay is a fundamental element of Grand Strategy Games and forms a large part of their commercial and educational appeal.

Because of this free form play, there is no guarantee that the situation which prompted the crusades will develop within the game. The carefully curated databases of characters and land holdings within *Crusader Kings II* allow play from as early as 769, long before the emergence of crusade ideology, and from this point of divergence it is perfectly possible for a vastly different geo-political situation to emerge by the end of the eleventh century. The *Civilization* series, which uses randomised maps and a very abstract model of religion, can allow for even more divergent outcomes: Jerusalem, Christianity, or Islam may not exist; the most holy city of Christianity may be Beijing; or the concept of Crusade may be embraced by Taoism.

From an academic perspective the possible absence of the crusades within a game spanning the Middle Ages is not an issue. The main educational and scholarly value of structural simulations is their ability to present explanations of the factors behind events rather than meticulously reconstructing the past.[29] If causes for the crusades don't emerge, it follows that the crusades should not occur. If the game mechanics allow for the possibility of the crusades under certain circumstances, the absence of these events in a particular playthrough does not negate the academic or learning value of the game.

However, this situation is problematic for commercial game designers who are ultimately constrained by the expense of modelling the crusades.[30] New game assets are required such as models for military units. Deeper representations of the crusades require the modification of mechanics or creation of entirely new gameplay elements to allow and encourage the player and computer-controlled actors to engage in these expeditions and to deal with the new geo-political situation they create. Preparing a detailed rendering of the crusades requires the commitment of substantial time and resources,[31] and this is difficult to justify unless they will occur in most games.

This tension is exacerbated by player expectations of the representation of the crusades. There is substantial demand for the inclusion of the crusades within strategy games set in the Middle Ages. Further, there is substantial demand for games portraying this period (and history more generally) to be 'historically accurate'.[32] Players' understanding of 'historical accuracy' varies substantially between individuals, but often centres around events within a game unfolding in a manner similar to that in the real world.

Players therefore expect crusades to occur within their games and for these expeditions to focus primarily (if not solely) on the Holy Land.

These factors place conflicting demands on the creators of these games. Grand Strategy Games allow player agency as part of their core appeal and so need to allow the possibility that the events which instigated the crusades will not occur. But the work required to adequately portray the events of the crusades and player expectation of how the crusades should be depicted demands the curtailment of that agency: if the crusades are modelled in depth through the game, then player actions must not be allowed to disrupt this core element. Designers have addressed this issue in several ways, but each of these marginalise the causes of the crusades. The *Civilization* series avoids the problem through its abstract representation of religion as a whole,[33] which uses the crusades as flavour for the medieval period rather than a substantial set of mechanics. *Medieval: Total War* presents the crusades as distinct events with their own mechanics, but ensures that they will occur by limiting players' agency. *Crusader Kings II* makes use of a dynamic set of triggers to instigate the crusades but provides a very limited explanation for their causes: they will happen automatically if certain key cities such as Rome or Constantinople are held by non-Christians after a certain point in the game. The developers of these games dedicated substantial time and effort in constructing the mechanics and audio-visual resources which support their presentation of the crusades and need to be certain that the majority of players will be able to engage with these mechanics. For this to happen, the crusades must occur in almost every playthrough and so the causes of the crusade must be presented in an arbitrary manner.

## Participants in the crusades

Within Grand Strategy Games the crusades are almost invariably presented as driven by the great rulers of Christendom: the Emperor in Germany and the kings of Europe. These figures are shown dictating the targets of crusades, commanding armies in the field, and ultimately gaining control of conquered territories. Lesser magnates such as dukes or counts are generally marginalised or ignored outright.

Again, this simplified presentation is problematic for scholarly discussion of the crusades. The participants on the crusades were diverse. While several crusades were led by kings and emperors, secular magnates from across Europe invariably played a decisive role.[34] Bishops and other clergy participated, acting as sacral support but also in a logistical or even military capacity.[35] The Italian maritime cities supported expeditions.[36]

This discrepancy is largely a consequence of the centring of kingdoms and their rulers as the driving force of history within these games and consequent marginalisation or absence of other figures. The *Civilization* series typically provides around 6,000 years of play, but the player acts as a single totemic ruler throughout this period. *Medieval: Total War* provides a superficial representation of dynastic rule, but ultimately the ruler and their family are present only in support of the mechanics of the kingdom. This focus on polities as player characters restricts play to the highest levels of society so there is no opportunity to experience *Civilization* or *Medieval: Total War* as the Count of Toulouse or similar magnate. There are clear design and accessibility factors behind this approach, but restricting play to the rulers of medieval realms in this way creates a fundamental problem when these games address the crusades. As there are no autonomous magnates, the crusades in these games must be led by kings. Events similar to the First Crusade or Fourth Crusade, driven by powerful magnates rather than the rulers of kingdoms,[37] cannot happen.

This king-centric gameplay also stymies games' representations of the Crusader States and casts them invariably as directly ruled colonies of their home kingdoms. As these games do not include magnates in their crusades, they have no ability to detail the political and cultural complexities of the kingdoms created in the wake of the crusades. For example, a successful crusade in *Medieval: Total War* results in the creation of an enclave in the Holy Land (or occasionally elsewhere) ruled and administered directly from the home kingdom. Any Crusader States created through the course of the game will be colonies of a single European power. They will be drawn inexorably into the conflicts of their European ruler and their economic and military resources will be channelled back to this home kingdom.

This model of the Crusader States as proto-colonies conforms to scholarship common throughout most of the nineteenth century, first as a defence of modern colonial claims to the Middle East and as part of the nationalist discourse of Western Europe, then as a condemnation of colonialism in the region and means of legitimising the nations (both Arab and Israeli) which emerged after the second world war.[38] More recently, various terrorist factions including ISIS and Al-Qaeda have equated Israel with the Crusader States and hence with Western colonialist activity.[39]

While the polities constructed by the first crusaders certainly displayed some modern colonial traits and characteristics, most recent scholarship underlines the shortcomings of this model. The Crusader States were certainly supported militarily and financially by the European kingdoms and could often be influenced by the rulers of these entities but, unlike modern colonies, they were functionally independent, their rulers were drawn from diverse kingdoms and regions with no single obvious colonial overlord,[40] and they did not channel resources back to their kingdoms of origin.[41] The distinction is important, but lost in the representations within most games. The Crusader States were certainly products of violence and conquest, their creation was undeniably accompanied by a number of atrocities, and in a broad sense they may be considered a form of 'colony'. However, equating them with modern-era colonies and modern colonialism undermines our understanding of both phenomena.

Even *Crusader Kings II*, which includes characters from broader social strata, struggles with these issues. The game models a rudimentary feudal system, allowing play over four societal levels (Emperor, King, Duke, and Count) and including computer actors at two further levels (Baron, Unlanded). Most of these characters are vassals of some sort and a substantial part of the game mechanics address the horizontal and vertical socio-political interaction of this array of figures. This model allows the presentation of crusades led by dukes or counts, but in practice, most crusades in *Crusader Kings II* are dominated by kings and result in the establishment of a home-ruled colony – even a magnate led expedition results in the creation of a mono-cultured kingdom ruled alongside lands in Europe.

## Objectives of the crusades

The motivation to crusade within Grand Strategy Games is almost inevitably the expansion of the player's domain. Although these games often include other mechanical and narrative elements to encourage the player to embark on crusade in the form of beneficial character traits, additional free military units, or more abstract rewards such as piety and prestige, conquest remains by far the most visible motivating factor.

This is a vast oversimplification of the diverse and changing motivations of the majority of crusaders.[42] These nuances are hard to identify with any degree of certainty, but it is implausible that all the participants on these expeditions held a unified and persistent goal.[43] Although some crusaders such as Bohemond of Taranto or Baldwin of Boulogne openly sought personal conquest,[44] it is almost certain that the majority of crusaders did not share this goal. It seems that pope Urban II initially planned to return Jerusalem to the hands of the Byzantine Emperor, rather than any of the participants,[45] thus realising the grand plans of Gregory VII.[46] At the very least, while the expedition was certainly intended to conquer lands, there was no clear idea about what to do with these lands once they were conquered.[47]

Furthermore, very few crusaders remained in the Holy Land.[48] Crusaders such as Robert Curthose, Hugh of Vermandois, and Stephen of Blois held substantial lands in Europe and demonstrably intended to return to these territories.[49] As Jotischky suggests, even those crusaders such as Raymond of Toulouse and Godfrey of Boullion who did settle in the Levant did not necessarily intend to do this when they took the cross: accounts of them giving up their lands prior to leaving for Jerusalem are retrospective and may represent the revision of events to better suit the narrative of legitimacy and piety claimed by these figures and their successors.[50] While the first crusaders were certainly concerned with conquest, for most participants this conquest was not for personal gain. Participants on subsequent expeditions to the East seem to have followed this broad pattern: they may have aimed to extend the territories of the Crusader States, but they seldom sought to acquire lands for themselves.

Instead the majority of crusaders must have been compelled to crusade by other factors. The promise of indulgence provided moral motivation.[51] Crusading could be politically opportune: the clusters of minor lords who accompanied their neighbouring great magnates may have sought stronger connections with these powerful figures,[52] and these magnates took a substantial portion of their vassals with them.[53] Emperor Henry IV seems to have attempted to assert his authority through his abortive commitment to a penitential war in the East in 1103 which made no mention of his rival Pope Paschal II.[54] Family groups often crusaded together, and family tradition and connections certainly played a role in motivating later crusaders, including the extensive network of northern French magnates which came to rule over much of the Crusader States.[55] The prospect of plunder and prestige may have motivated some crusaders on every expedition,[56] although the costs involved in crusading surely limited their viability as profit turning ventures.[57] While the involvement of the Italian merchant cities seems to have been primarily motivated through piety, the expansion of trade routes may have also been a motivating factor.[58]

These complex and varied motivations are ignored or marginalised in favour of simple expansion of personal territory because the underlying nature of Grand Strategy Games demands or at least encourages conquest and domination through their victory conditions.[59] Even games with multiple paths to victory such as *Civilization* almost inevitably include world conquest as an option, and typically this is the easiest or otherwise most attractive approach.[60] These violent tendencies are actively encouraged through the design of most Grand Strategy Games: in many cases the vast majority of game mechanics focus on warfare or activities in support of warfare.[61] *Medieval: Total War* is a particularly clear example of this tendency with its focus on real-time battles. This tendency towards violent expansion is so endemic to the genre that it influences player expectations and behaviour even in Grand Strategy Games which discourage warfare.[62] As economics, religion, and diplomacy are peripheral to this focus on armed expansion, it is unsurprising that crusades are presented as another tool to this end.

## *Holy Fury*

*Holy Fury* addresses some of the issues discussed above and provides perhaps the most developed presentation of the crusades in digital games. Game mechanics have been introduced or modified to more closely reflect the broad motivations of crusaders and the complex and fragmented states they created. The territorial rewards for crusading are curtailed. Players may still choose to claim the crusade target for themselves, but they are encouraged to select an unlanded beneficiary from within their family as the independent recipient of the spoils of conquest. This installation of relatives is the assumed process for artificial intelligence-controlled (AI) actors and moves away from the model of crusading for the sake of personal territorial expansion.

Beyond this, a successful crusade no longer leaves its most active participant in sole control of the new kingdom and able to distribute its lands to his followers freely. Instead, the lands of the kingdom are distributed amongst the beneficiaries of each of its members. The aftermath of a victorious crusade to Jerusalem now typically results in the new king of Jerusalem controlling only the area immediately around the city with the rest of region from Sinai to Tripoli in the hands of his new vassals: a diverse range of incoming magnates. Each of these figures brings the baggage of pre-existing loyalties, rivalries, and ambitions from their European dynasties. Additional independent Crusader States similar to the County of Edessa or Principality of Antioch may be established during the crusade itself. The result of these changes is an independent and fractious kingdom much closer in composition and politics to the actual Crusader States.

Perhaps more importantly, the scope of non-territorial rewards has been extended substantially. Participants on a crusade now receive a portion of the 'War Chest' comprising gold and relics donated by Christian magnates which means the expeditions can now be a lucrative means of gaining wealth, piety, and prestige. Participants in crusades may earn 'Crusader Bloodlines' which provide a range of bonuses to the character and their descendants. These rewards are abstract and not always rooted in reality, but nevertheless present a broader range of motivations for the crusaders.

However, although *Holy Fury* presents a more nuanced vision of the crusades, there are still shortcomings within its model. Most significantly there is no explanation for the causes of the movement as providing more detailed mechanics here could prevent the crusades from occurring at all. The culturally and politically complex Crusader States which emerge within the game are an important development, but these polities are still based around the limitations of the game's feudal model. Providing a greater range of motivations to crusades beyond territorial acquisition is likewise significant, but its success appears to be limited as players of the game still tend towards territorial expansion above all else.

## Conclusion

Creators seeking to represent the crusades through Grand Strategy Games face a number of fundamental issues as a consequence of the nature of the genre and the expectations of its players. The degree of player agency typical within these games in combination with the resources required to portray them leads designers to ignore the causes of these events to ensure that they occur in each playthrough. The limitation of player and computer-controlled actors to the level of kings and emperors presents an abstract and substantially limited representation of a crusade movement dominated and led by monarchs and the Crusader States as a series of anachronistic colonies ruled directly from their home kingdoms. The tendency within Grand Strategy Games and amongst their playerbase to focus on personal conquest and military domination over every other aspect of rulership distorts and simplifies the motivations of the crusaders.

To address these issues and create a more nuanced and considered representation of the crusades it is necessary to reconsider the core elements of Grand Strategy Games and our expectations of them while retaining their ability to engage with complex historical issues in a deep and thoughtful manner. The developers of *Holy Fury* have addressed some of these issues to a certain extent through the modification of the mechanics of *Crusader Kings II*, and have created a more thorough exploration of the crusades as a result. The result is impressive and highly laudable. But their efforts have been hampered by the underlying mechanics of the genre, and the expectations of the game's players. In *Holy Fury* the crusades remain an isolated modification of the core rules of the game rather than a part of a dedicated model constructed from the ground up.

Most fundamentally then, crusades must form an integral element of a game's mechanics. They should not appear as an abrupt and unexplained change to gameplay. Nor should they exist as a scripted series of pre-ordained events. The causes of the crusades need to be considered in more depth and this will require modelling of Church reform, papal and imperial rhetoric, relationships between Western and Eastern Christianity and their leaders, and a range of other factors. This will allow the player to interact with the various elements presented through the game and to explore the causes of the crusades by adjusting these elements and experiencing different outcomes.

This interactivity and player agency presents the possibility that the crusades will not take place in every playthrough and this necessitates a different design approach. Resources should not be focused solely on the representation of the crusades themselves, and their military elements in particular, but rather should be distributed more evenly across the themes and issues which are connected to the crusades more broadly. The crusades should be modelled as part of a broader consideration of religious change and global relationships. This wider distribution of mechanics and supporting assets could substantially mitigate any concerns about wasted resources from crusades which didn't happen.

A more substantial mechanical division between character and territory could help to resolve the restrictive issues around the portrayal of the participants in the crusades and their motivations within Grand Strategy Games. The ability to play as a character without a defined landholding could ease the movement of figures from Europe to the Crusader States and could better represent powerful magnates relinquishing their European lands to facilitate their expeditions. This could be accompanied by a shift to a more roleplay-orientated model could provide additional motivation for characters to embark on crusade.

A change in objectives away from global domination would also be beneficial in explaining the motivations of crusaders.[63] The benefits of crusading beyond territorial acquisition presented in *Holy Fury* could be expanded. Victory conditions other than conquest could be introduced. Beneficial or challenge objectives could be created in the form of missions rewarding the player for participating in a crusade without acquiring lands.

This analysis highlights more general difficulties faced by creators of Grand Strategy Games dealing with the Middle Ages or history more broadly. There are fundamental limitations in the use of the same simple abstract mechanics to model events over a broad chronological or geographic scope. As a result, while wide-ranging games like *Civilization* can certainly be useful, more narrow but deeper explorations of a particular period or event could be of scholarly value in different ways. Violence and warfare remain at the heart of almost all Grand Strategy Games, but this often undermines their representation of the past. Likewise, a focus on roleplaying individuals rather than commanding a polity as a faceless omnipotent ruler could allow for a deeper representation of many historical events, allowing a more vibrant exploration of the past.

Beyond the educational benefits, a more thorough and focused representation of the crusades could be commercially attractive and may help to create more entertaining games for a particular audience. Although the most vocal demands for historical authenticity in games relate to the veracity of material culture,[64] a substantial section of the playerbase of Grand Strategy Games is concerned with the way in which a game presents historical arguments through its mechanics and objectives. There is therefore a potential for more detailed games to command a large audience – as evidenced by the large following of the various *Paradox Interactive* games. A shift in game mechanics may engage new users and could provide a different experience for existing players. The effort behind *Holy Fury* is demonstrative of a willingness among commercial game companies to invest in the production of games which provide a deep consideration of the crusades and the success of the expansion suggests a substantial demand for this approach. *Holy Fury* is limited by the mechanical framework in which it was created, but is indicative of a broader trend towards more diverse representations of the crusades and the Middle Ages more generally. Likewise, the emergence of new approaches to medieval rulership and politics in games outside the Grand Strategy genre such as *Mount and Blade* and *Reigns* highlight the possibilities of this medium. Digital games have substantial potential as tools for interacting with the medieval world and these developments may allow more expression of the role of medieval monarchs, not only as rulers of kingdoms, but as crusader kings too.

## Notes

1 Ernest Adams, *Fundamentals of Game Design* (Berkeley, CA: New Riders, 2014), 423.
2 Robert Houghton, "Where Did You Learn That? The Self-Perceived Educational Impact of Historical Computer Games on Undergraduates," *Gamevironments* 5 (2016): 26–27.
3 Adam Chapman, "Is Sid Meier's Civilization History?" *Rethinking History* 17, no. 3 (2013): 318.
4 Adam Chapman, *Digital Games as History: How Videogames Represent the Past and Offer Access to Historical Practice*, Routledge Advances in Game Studies 7 (New York, NY: Routledge, 2016), 71–73.
5 Niall Ferguson, ed., *Virtual History: Alternatives and Counterfactuals* (New York, NY: Basic Books, 2001), 89; William Uricchio, "Simulation, History, and Computer Games," in *Handbook of Computer Game Studies*, ed. Joost Raessens and Jeffrey Haskell Goldstein (Cambridge, MA: MIT Press, 2005), 328; Harry J Brown, *Videogames and Education* (Armonk, NY: M. E. Sharpe, 2008), 118;

Rolfe Daus Peterson, Andrew Justin Miller, and Sean Joseph Fedorko, "The Same River Twice: Exploring Historical Representation and the Value of Simulation in the Total War, Civilization and Patrician Franchises," in *Playing with the Past: Digital Games and the Simulation of History*, ed. Matthew Kapell and Andrew B. R. Elliott (New York, NY: Bloomsbury, 2013), esp. 38; Chapman, *Digital Games as History*, 231–57.

6  Christopher Douglas, "'You Have Unleashed a Horde of Barbarians!': Fighting Indians, Playing Games, Forming Disciplines," *Postmodern Culture* 13, no. 1 (2002); Claudio Fogu, "Digitizing Historical Consciousness," *History and Theory* 48, no. 2 (2009): 118; Adam Chapman, "Affording History: Civilization and the Ecological Epproach," in *Playing with the Past: Digital Games and the Simulation of History*, ed. Matthew Kapell and Andrew B. R. Elliott (New York, NY: Bloomsbury, 2013), 67; Jeremiah McCall, "Simulation Games and the Study of the Past: Classroom Guidelines," in *Pastplay*, ed. Kevin Kee (Ann Arbor, MI: University of Michigan Press, 2014), 229–30.

7  Andrew McMichael, "PC Games and the Teaching of History," *The History Teacher* 40, no. 2 (February 2007): 203–18; John K. Lee and Jeffrey Probert, "Civilization III and Whole-Class Play," *The Journal of Social Studies Research* 34, no. 1 (2010): 1–28; John Pagnotti and William B. Russell, "Using Civilization IV to Engage Students in World History Content," *The Social Studies* 103, no. 1 (2012): 39–48; McCall, "Simulation Games and the Study of the Past"; Stephen Ortega, "Representing the Past: Video Games Challenge to the Historical Narrative," *Syllabus* 4, no. 1 (2015): 1–13.

8  Jeremiah McCall, "Playing with the Past: History and Video Games (and Why It Might Matter)," *Journal of Geek Studies* 6, no. 1 (2019): 39.

9  Douglas, "You Have Unleashed a Horde of Barbarians!"; Emily Joy Bembeneck, "Phantasms of Rome: Video Games and Cultural Identity," in *Playing with the Past: Digital Games and the Simulation of History*, ed. Matthew Kapell and Andrew B. R. Elliott (New York, NY, 2013), 77–90; Rebecca Mir and Trevor Owens, "Modeling Indigenous Peoples: Unpacking Ideology in Sid Meier's Colonization," in *Playing with the Past: Digital Games and the Simulation of History*, ed. Matthew Kapell and Andrew B. R. Elliott (New York, NY, 2013), 91–106; Ortega, "Representing the Past," 3; Dom Ford, "'EXplore, EXpand, EXploit, Exterminate': Affective Writing of Postcolonial History and Education in Civilization V," *Game Studies* 16, no. 2 (2017).

10 Kaspar Pobłocki, "Becoming-State: The Bio-Cultural Imperialism of Sid Meier's Civilization," *Focaal – European Journal of Anthropology* 39 (2002): 163–77; McCall, "Playing with the Past," 41–42.

11 Alex Whelchel, "Using Civilization Simulation Video Games in the World History Classroom," *World History Connected* 4, no. 2 (2007): 117; Ortega, "Representing the Past," 2; Ford, "'EXplore, EXpand, EXploit, Exterminate'."

12 Jeremiah McCall, "Navigating the Problem Space: The Medium of Simulation Games in the Teaching of History," *History Teacher* 1 (2012): 17.

13 Robert Houghton, "World, Structure and Play: A Framework for Games as Historical Research Outputs, Tools, and Processes," *Práticas Da História* 7 (2018): 24.

14 Giles Constable, "The Second Crusade as Seen by Contemporaries," *Traditio* 9 (1953): 213–79; Jonathan Riley-Smith, *What Were the Crusades?* (Basingstoke: Palgrave Macmillan, 2009), ix; Jonathan Phillips, *The Second Crusade:*

*Extending the Frontiers of Christendom* (New Haven, CT: Yale University Press, 2010), 228–68.
15 H. E. Mayer, *The Crusades* (Oxford: Oxford University Press, 1988).
16 Ernst-Dieter Hehl, "Was Ist Eigentlich Ein Kreuzzug?" *Historische Zeitschrift* 259, no. 1 (1994).
17 Giles Constable, "The Historiography of the Crusades," in *The Crusades from the Perspective of Byzantium and the Muslim World*, ed. Angeliki E. Laiou and Roy P. Mottahedeh (Washington, DC: Dumbarton Oaks Research Library and Collection, 2001): 1–22; Christopher Tyerman, *The Debate on the Crusades*, Issues in Historiography (Manchester: Manchester University Press, 2011), 218–28.
18 Uricchio, "Simulation, History, and Computer Games," 328; Alexander R. Galloway, *Gaming: Essays on Algorithmic Culture*, Electronic Mediations 18 (Minneapolis, MI, 2006), 104; Jeremiah McCall, "Historical Simulations as Problem Spaces: Criticism and Classroom Use," *Journal of Digital Humanities* 1, no. 2 (2012).
19 Adam Smith and Soren Johnson, "Soren Johnson on Challenging the Norms of 4X Games," *Rock, Paper, Shotgun* [blog], June 4, 2018, www.rockpapershotgun.com/2018/04/06/soren-johnson-4x-strategy-interview/, accessed December 12, 2018.
20 Chang, "Love Is in the Air: Queer (Im)Possibility and Straightwashing in FrontierVille and World of Warcraft," *QED: A Journal in GLBTQ Worldmaking* 2, no. 2 (2015): 27–29.
21 Chapman, *Digital Games as History*, 37–39; Andrew B. R. Elliott, "Simulations and Simulacra: History in Video Games," *Práticas Da História* 5 (2017): 19; Houghton, "World, Structure and Play," 27–31; Robert Houghton, "Scholarly History through Digital Games: Pedagogical Practice as Research Method," *The Interactive Pasts* 2 (2020).
22 H. E. J. Cowdrey, "The Peace and the Truce of God in the Eleventh Century," *Past and Present* 46 (1970): 42–67; Ernst-Dieter Hehl, *Kirche und Krieg im 12. Jahrhundert: Studien zu kanon. Recht u. polit. Wirklichkeit*, Monographien zur Geschichte des Mittelalters 19 (Stuttgart: Hiersemann, 1980); John France, *Victory in the East: A Military History of the First Crusade* (Cambridge: Cambridge University Press, 1994), 7–9; Jonathan Riley-Smith, *The First Crusaders, 1095–1131* (Cambridge: Cambridge University Press, 1997), 6, 40–52; Jean Richard, *The Crusades, c. 1071–c. 1291* (Cambridge: Cambridge University Press, 1999), 10; Andrew Jotischky, *Crusading and the Crusader States* (Harlow: Pearson, 2004), 5; Jonathan Riley-Smith, *The First Crusade and the Idea of Crusading* (London: Continuum, 2009), 16–17.
23 France, *Victory in the East*, 6–7; Riley-Smith, *The First Crusaders*, 23–39.
24 Jotischky, *Crusading and the Crusader States*, 23–30.
25 Ferguson, *Virtual History*, 89; Uricchio, "Simulation, History, and Computer Games," 328; Brown, *Videogames and Education*, 118; Peterson et al., "The Same River Twice," esp. 38; Chapman, *Digital Games as History*, 231–57.
26 McCall, "Historical Simulations as Problem Spaces."
27 Peterson et al., "The Same River Twice," 43.
28 Robert Houghton, "If You're Going to Be the King, You'd Better Damn Well Act like the King: Setting Objectives to Encourage Realistic Play in Grand Strategy Computer Games," in *The Middle Ages in Modern Culture: History*

and *Authenticity in Contemporary Medievalism*, ed. Karl Alvestad and Robert Houghton (New York, NY: I. B. Tauris, 2020).
29 Peterson et al., "The Same River Twice," 38.
30 Jeremiah McCall, "Video Games as Participatory Public History," in *A Companion to Public History*, 1st ed., ed. D. M. Dean (Hoboken, NJ: Wiley, 2018), 407; Houghton, "World, Structure and Play," 35–36.
31 Timothy Compeau and Robert MacDougall, "Tecumseh Lies Here: Goals and Challenges for a Pervasive History Game in Progress," in *Pastplay: Teaching and Learning History with Technology*, ed. Kevin Kee (Ann Arbor, MI: University of Michigan Press, 2014), 98.
32 Erik Champion, *Critical Gaming: Interactive History and Virtual Heritage*, Digital Research in the Arts and Humanities (Farnham, 2015); Tara Jane Copplestone, "But That's Not Accurate: The Differing Perceptions of Accuracy in Cultural-Heritage Videogames between Creators, Consumers and Critics," *Rethinking History* 21, no. 3 (2017): 430–33.
33 Vit Šisler, "From Kuma\War to Quraish: Representation of Islam in Arab and American Video Games," in *Playing with Religion in Digital Games*, ed. Heidi Campbell and Gregory P. Grieve, Digital Game Studies (Bloomington, IN: Indiana University Press, 2014), 124–25.
34 Marcus Bull, "The Roots of Lay Enthusiasm for the First Crusade," in *The Crusades: The Essential Readings*, ed. Thomas F. Madden, Blackwell Essential Readings in History (Oxford: Blackwell, 2002), 173–93; John France, "Patronage and the Appeal of the First Crusade," in *The Crusades: The Essential Readings*, ed. Thomas F. Madden, Blackwell Essential Readings in History (Oxford: Blackwell, 2002), 195–207.
35 Janet L. Nelson, "The Church's Military Service in the Ninth Century: A Contemporary Comparative View?," *Studies in Church History* 20 (1983): 29; Philippe Contamine, *War in the Middle Ages*, trans. Michael Jones (New York, NY: Blackwell, 1984), 60.
36 Robert Henri Bautier, *The Economic Development of Medieval Europe* (London: Thames and Hudson, 1971), 101–7; France, *Victory in the East*, 15; Riley-Smith, *The First Crusaders*, 17; John H. Pryor, "The Venetian Fleet for the Fourth Crusade and the Diversion of the Crusade to Constantinople," in *The Experience of Crusading*, ed. Marcus Graham Bull et al. (Cambridge: Cambridge University Press, 2003), 60–79.
37 Jotischky, *Crusading and the Crusader States*, 55–56.
38 Riley-Smith, *The First Crusaders*, 15–16; Jotischky, *Crusading and the Crusader States*, 16–19; Ronnie Ellenblum, *Crusader Castles and Modern Histories* (Cambridge: Cambridge University Press, 2007), 18–61; Tyerman, *The Debate on the Crusades*, 125–81; Kristen Skottki, "The Dead, the Revived and the Recreated Pasts: 'Structural Amnesia' in Representations of Crusade History," in *Perceptions of the Crusades from the Nineteenth to the Twenty-First Century*, ed. Mike Horswell and Jonathan Phillips, Engaging the Crusades: The Memory and Legacy of Crusading (Abingdon: Routledge, 2018), 109–32.
39 Skottki, "The Dead, the Revived and the Recreated Pasts," 114; Tyerman, *The Debate on the Crusades*, 235–42; Akil N. Awan, "Weaponising the Crusades: Justifying Terrorism and Political Violence," in *The Crusades in the Modern World*, ed. Mike Horswell and Akil N. Awan, Engaging the Crusades, volume 2 (Abingdon: Routledge, 2020), 4–17.

*Crusader kings too?* 87

40 Joshua Prawer, *The Crusaders' Kingdom: European Colonialism in the Middle Ages* (London: Phoenix Press, 2001), 61–63.
41 Jotischky, *Crusading and the Crusader States*, 19–20.
42 France, *Victory in the East*, 16.
43 Jotischky, *Crusading and the Crusader States*, 16.
44 Riley-Smith, *The First Crusaders*, 18; Jotischky, *Crusading and the Crusader States*, 13–14.
45 H. E. J. Cowdrey, "Pope Gregory VII's 'Crusading' Plans," in *Outremer: Studies in the History of the Crusading Kingdom of Jerusalem*, ed. B. Z. Kedar, H. E. Mayer, and R. C. Smail (Jerusalem: Yad Izhak Ben-Zvi Institute, 1982), 27–40; France, *Victory in the East*, 4; Jonathan Riley-Smith, "Early Crusaders to the East and the Costs of Crusading, 1095–1130," in *The Crusades: The Essential Readings*, ed. Thomas F. Madden, Blackwell Essential Readings in History (Oxford: Blackwell, 2002), esp. 171; Jotischky, *Crusading and the Crusader States*, 62; Riley-Smith, *The First Crusade*, 21–22.
46 Riley-Smith, *The First Crusaders*, 50.
47 Ibid., 6; Jotischky, *Crusading and the Crusader States*, 62.
48 Riley-Smith, *The First Crusaders*, 14, 18–19; Jotischky, *Crusading and the Crusader States*, 13–14.
49 Jotischky, *Crusading and the Crusader States*, 14.
50 Ibid.
51 Marcus Graham Bull, *Knightly Piety and the Lay Response to the First Crusade: The Limousin and Gascony, c. 970–c. 1130* (Oxford: Clarendon Press, 1993); France, *Victory in the East*, 10–11; Riley-Smith, *The First Crusaders*, 83–84; Richard, *The Crusades*, 15–18; Bull, "The Roots of Lay Enthusiasm for the First Crusade"; Christopher Marshall, "The Crusading Motivation of the Italian City Republics in the Latin East, 1096–1104," in *The Experience of Crusading*, ed. Marcus Graham Bull et al. (Cambridge: Cambridge University Press, 2003), 60–79; Phillips, *The Second Crusade*, 103–5.
52 Riley-Smith, *The First Crusaders*, 89–91.
53 Ibid., 88; Jotischky, *Crusading and the Crusader States*, 15–16; Phillips, *The Second Crusade*, 102–3.
54 Riley-Smith, *The First Crusaders*, 10.
55 Ibid., 7–8, 21–22, 93–105; Phillips, *The Second Crusade*, 99–101.
56 France, *Victory in the East*, 12–13; Riley-Smith, *The First Crusaders*, 146; France, "Patronage and the Appeal of the First Crusade"; Phillips, *The Second Crusade*, 105.
57 Riley-Smith, *The First Crusaders*, 8, 19–21, 106–43; Riley-Smith, "Early Crusaders to the East"; Norman Housley, "Costing the Crusade: Budgeting for Crusading Activity in the Fourteenth Century," in *The Experience of Crusading*, ed. Marcus Graham Bull et al. (Cambridge: Cambridge University Press, 2003), 45–59; Jotischky, *Crusading and the Crusader States*, 14–15.
58 Bautier, *The Economic Development of Medieval Europe*, 101–7; France, *Victory in the East*, 15; Riley-Smith, *The First Crusaders*, 17; Pryor, "The Venetian Fleet for the Fourth Crusade".
59 Pobłocki, "Becoming-State: The Bio-Cultural Imperialism of Sid Meier's Civilization"; McMichael, "PC Games and the Teaching of History," 214; Adams, *Fundamentals of Game Design*, 423.
60 McMichael, "PC Games and the Teaching of History," 214; Houghton, "If You're Going to Be the King."

61 Adams, *Fundamentals of Game Design*, 423.
62 Houghton, "If You're Going to Be the King."
63 Ibid.
64 Adam Chapman, "Privileging Form Over Content: Analysing Historical Videogames," *Journal of Digital Humanities* 1, no. 2 (2012): 42–46; Champion, *Critical Gaming*.

## Bibliography

Adams, Ernest. *Fundamentals of Game Design*. 3rd ed. Voices That Matter. Berkeley, CA: New Riders, 2014.

Awan, Akil N. "Weaponising the Crusades: Justifying Terrorism and Political Violence." In *The Crusades in the Modern World*, edited by Mike Horswell and Akil N. Awan, 4–17. Engaging the Crusades, Vol. 2. Abingdon: Routledge, 2020.

Bautier, Robert Henri. *The Economic Development of Medieval Europe*. London: Thames and Hudson, 1971.

Bembeneck, Emily Joy. "Phantasms of Rome: Video Games and Cultural Identity." In *Playing with the Past: Digital Games and the Simulation of History*, edited by Matthew Kapell and Andrew B. R. Elliott, 77–90. New York, NY: Bloomsbury, 2013.

Brown, Harry J. *Videogames and Education*. Armonk, NY: M. E. Sharpe, 2008.

Bull, Marcus. *Knightly Piety and the Lay Response to the First Crusade: The Limousin and Gascony, c. 970-c. 1130*. Oxford: Clarendon Press, 1993.

———. "The Roots of Lay Enthusiasm for the First Crusade." In *The Crusades: The Essential Readings*, edited by Thomas F. Madden, 173–93. Blackwell Essential Readings in History. Oxford: Blackwell, 2002.

Champion, Erik. *Critical Gaming: Interactive History and Virtual Heritage*. Digital Research in the Arts and Humanities. Farnham, Surrey: Ashgate, 2015.

Chang, Edmond Y. "Love is in the Air: Queer (Im)Possibility and Straightwashing in FrontierVille and World of Warcraft." *QED: A Journal in GLBTQ Worldmaking* 2, no. 2 (2015).

Chapman, Adam. "Affording History: Civilization and the Ecological Approach." In *Playing with the Past: Digital Games and the Simulation of History*, edited by Matthew Kapell and Andrew B. R. Elliott, 61–73. New York, NY: Bloomsbury, 2013.

———. *Digital Games as History: How Videogames Represent the Past and Offer Access to Historical Practice*. Routledge Advances in Game Studies 7. New York, NY: Routledge, 2016.

———. "Is Sid Meier's Civilization History?" *Rethinking History* 17, no. 3 (2013): 312–32.

———. "Privileging Form Over Content: Analysing Historical Videogames." *Journal of Digital Humanities* 1, no. 2 (2012): 42–46.

Compeau, Timothy, and Robert MacDougall. "Tecumseh Lies Here: Goals and Challenges for a Pervasive History Game in Progress." In *Pastplay: Teaching and Learning History with Technology*, edited by Kevin Kee, 87–108. Ann Arbor, MI: University of Michigan Press, 2014.

Constable, Giles. "The Historiography of the Crusades." In *The Crusades from the Perspective of Byzantium and the Muslim World*, edited by Angeliki E. Laiou and Roy P. Mottahedeh, 1–22. Washington, DC: Dumbarton Oaks Research Library and Collection, 2001.

———. "The Second Crusade as Seen by Contemporaries." *Traditio* 9 (1953): 213–79.

Contamine, Philippe. *War in the Middle Ages*. Translated by Michael Jones. New York, NY: Blackwell, 1984.

Copplestone, Tara Jane. "But that's not Accurate: The Differing Perceptions of Accuracy in Cultural-Heritage Videogames between Creators, Consumers and Critics." *Rethinking History* 21, no. 3 (2017): 415–38.

Cowdrey, H. E. J. "Pope Gregory VII's 'Crusading' Plans." In *Outremer: Studies in the History of the Crusading Kingdom of Jerusalem*, edited by B. Z. Kedar, H. E. Mayer, and R. C. Smail, 27–40. Jerusalem: Yad Izhak Ben-Zvi Institute, 1982.

———. "The Peace and the Truce of God in the Eleventh Century." *Past and Present* 46 (1970): 42–67.

Douglas, Christopher. "'You Have Unleashed a Horde of Barbarians!': Fighting Indians, Playing Games, Forming Disciplines." *Postmodern Culture* 13, no. 1 (2002).

Ellenblum, Ronnie. *Crusader Castles and Modern Histories*. Cambridge: Cambridge University Press, 2007.

Elliott, Andrew B. R. "Simulations and Simulacra: History in Video Games." *Práticas Da História* 5 (2017): 11–41.

Ferguson, Niall, ed. *Virtual History: Alternatives and Counterfactuals*. Repr. New York, NY: Basic Books, 2001.

Fogu, Claudio. "Digitizing Historical Consciousness." *History and Theory* 48, no. 2 (May 2009): 103–21.

Ford, Dom. "'EXplore, EXpand, EXploit, Exterminate': Affective Writing of Postcolonial History and Education in Civilization V." *Game Studies* 16, no. 2 (2017).

France, John. "Patronage and the Appeal of the First Crusade." In *The Crusades: The Essential Readings*, edited by Thomas F. Madden, 195–207. Blackwell Essential Readings in History. Oxford, UK and Malden, MA: Blackwell, 2002.

———. *Victory in the East: A Military History of the First Crusade*. Cambridge: Cambridge University Press, 1994.

Galloway, Alexander R. *Gaming: Essays on Algorithmic Culture*. Electronic Mediations 18. Minneapolis, MN: University of Minnesota Press, 2006.

Hehl, Ernst-Dieter. *Kirche und Krieg im 12. Jahrhundert: Studien zu kanon. Recht u. polit. Wirklichkeit*. Monographien zur Geschichte des Mittelalters 19. Stuttgart: Hiersemann, 1980.

———. "Was Ist Eigentlich Ein Kreuzzug?" *Historische Zeitschrift* 259, no. 1 (1994).

Houghton, Robert. "If You're Going to Be the King, You'd Better Damn Well Act Like the King: Setting Objectives to Encourage Realistic Play in Grand Strategy Computer Games." In *The Middle Ages in Modern Culture: History and Authenticity in Contemporary Medievalism*, edited by Karl Alvestad and Robert Houghton. New York, NY: I. B. Tauris, 2020.

———. "Scholarly History through Digital Games: Pedagogical Practice as Research Method." *The Interactive Pasts* 2 (2020).

———. "Where Did You Learn That? The Self-Perceived Educational Impact of Historical Computer Games on Undergraduates." *Gamevironments* 5 (2016): 8–45.

———. "World, Structure and Play: A Framework for Games as Historical Research Outputs, Tools, and Processes." *Práticas Da História* 7 (2018): 11–43.

Housley, Norman. "Costing the Crusade: Budgeting for Crusading Activity in the Fourteenth Century." In *The Experience of Crusading*, edited by Marcus Graham Bull, Norman Housley, P. W. Edbury, and Jonathan Phillips, 45–59. Cambridge: Cambridge University Press, 2003.

Jotischky, Andrew. *Crusading and the Crusader States*. 1st ed. Recovering the Past. Harlow: Pearson, 2004.

Lee, John K., and Jeffrey Probert. "Civilization III and Whole-Class Play." *The Journal of Social Studies Research* 34, no. 1 (2010): 1–28.

Marshall, Christopher. "The Crusading Motivation of the Italian City Republics in the Latin East, 1096–104." In *The Experience of Crusading*, edited by Marcus Graham Bull, Norman Housley, P. W. Edbury, and Jonathan Phillips, 60–79. Cambridge: Cambridge University Press, 2003.

Mayer, H. E. *The Crusades*. 2nd ed. Oxford: Oxford University Press, 1988.

McCall, Jeremiah. "Historical Simulations as Problem Spaces: Criticism and Classroom Use." *Journal of Digital Humanities* 1, no. 2 (2012).

———. "Navigating the Problem Space: The Medium of Simulation Games in the Teaching of History." *History Teacher* 1 (2012): 9–28.

———. "Playing with the Past: History and Video Games (and Why It Might Matter)." *Journal of Geek Studies* 6, no. 1 (2019): 29–48.

———. "Simulation Games and the Study of the Past: Classroom Guidelines." In *Pastplay: Teaching and Learning History with Technology*, edited by Kevin Kee, 228–54. Ann Arbor, MI: University of Michigan Press, 2014.

———. "Video Games as Participatory Public History." In *A Companion to Public History*, 1st ed., edited by D. M. Dean, 405–16. Hoboken, NJ: Wiley, 2018.

McMichael, Andrew. "PC Games and the Teaching of History." *The History Teacher* 40, no. 2 (2007): 203–18.

Mir, Rebecca, and Trevor Owens. "Modeling Indigenous Peoples: Unpacking Ideology in Sid Meier's Colonization." In *Playing with the Past: Digital Games and the Simulation of History*, edited by Matthew Kapell and Andrew B. R. Elliott, 91–106. New York, NY: Bloomsbury, 2013.

Nelson, Janet L. "The Church's Military Service in the Ninth Century: A Contemporary Comparative View?" *Studies in Church History* 20 (1983): 15–30.

Ortega, Stephen. "Representing the Past: Video Games Challenge to the Historical Narrative." *Syllabus* 4, no. 1 (2015): 1–13.

Pagnotti, John, and William B. Russell. "Using Civilization IV to Engage Students in World History Content." *The Social Studies* 103, no. 1 (January 2012): 39–48.

Peterson, Rolfe Daus, Andrew Justin Miller, and Sean Joseph Fedorko. "The Same River Twice: Exploring Historical Representation and the Value of Simulation in the Total War, Civilization and Patrician Franchises." In *Playing with the Past: Digital Games and the Simulation of History*, edited by Matthew Kapell and Andrew B. R. Elliott, 33–48. New York, NY: Bloomsbury, 2013.

Phillips, Jonathan. *The Second Crusade: Extending the Frontiers of Christendom*. New Haven, CT: Yale University Press, 2010.

Pobłocki, Kaspar. "Becoming-State: The Bio-Cultural Imperialism of Sid Meier's Civilization." *Focaal – European Journal of Anthropology* 39 (2002): 163–77.

Prawer, Joshua. *The Crusaders' Kingdom: European Colonialism in the Middle Ages*. London: Phoenix Press, 2001.

Pryor, John H. "The Venetian Fleet for the Fourth Crusade and the Diversion of the Crusade to Constantinople." In *The Experience of Crusading*, edited by Marcus Graham Bull, Norman Housley, P. W. Edbury, and Jonathan Phillips, 60–79. Cambridge: Cambridge University Press, 2003.

Richard, Jean. *The Crusades, c. 1071–c. 1291*. Cambridge Medieval Textbooks. Cambridge: Cambridge University Press, 1999.

Riley-Smith, Jonathan. "Early Crusaders to the East and the Costs of Crusading, 1095–1130." In *The Crusades: The Essential Readings*, edited by Thomas F. Madden, 156–71. Blackwell Essential Readings in History. Oxford: Blackwell, 2002.

———. *The First Crusaders, 1095–1131*. Cambridge: Cambridge University Press, 1997.

———. *The First Crusade and the Idea of Crusading*. London: Continuum, 2009.

———. *What Were the Crusades?* Basingstoke: Palgrave Macmillan, 2009.

Šisler, Vít. "From Kuma\War to Quraish: Representation of Islam in Arab and American Video Games." In *Playing with Religion in Digital Games*, edited by Heidi Campbell and Gregory P. Grieve, 109–33. Digital Game Studies. Bloomington, IN: Indiana University Press, 2014.

Skottki, Kristen. "The Dead, the Revived and the Recreated Pasts: 'Structural Amnesia' in Representations of Crusade History." In *Perceptions of the Crusades from the Nineteenth to the Twenty-First Century*, 1st ed., edited by Mike Horswell and Jonathan Phillips, 109–32. Engaging the Crusades: The Memory and Legacy of Crusading. London: Routledge, 2018.

Smith, Adam, and Soren Johnson. "Soren Johnson on Challenging the Norms of 4X Games." *Rock, Paper, Shotgun* [blog], June 4, 2018. www.rockpapershotgun.com/2018/04/06/soren-johnson-4x-strategy-interview/. Accessed December 12, 2018.

Tyerman, Christopher. *The Debate on the Crusades*. Issues in Historiography. Manchester: Manchester University Press, 2011.
Uricchio, William. "Simulation, History, and Computer Games." In *Handbook of Computer Game Studies*, edited by Joost Raessens and Jeffrey Haskell Goldstein, 327–38. Cambridge, MA: MIT Press, 2005.
Whelchel, Alex. "Using Civilization Simulation Video Games in the World History Classroom." *World History Connected* 4, no. 2 (2007).

# 5 Learning to think historically

## Some theoretical challenges when playing the crusades

*Andreas Körber, Johannes Meyer-Hamme, and Robert Houghton*

It is a phenomenon of our time that computer games which use historical themes have introduced a large number of people to historical narratives. At least for certain groups, computer games can now be described as the leading medium of historical culture and have long since outstripped historical feature films. This is particularly true when considering the crusades; games like *Stronghold Crusader*, *Pilgrim: Faith as a Weapon*, *Assassin's Creed*, or *Anno 1404* enjoy audiences in the millions. The references made by computer games to the history of the crusades are diverse, as can be seen across the contributions to this volume.[1]

The ways in which these games appeal to players' historical identities and how they simultaneously rely on, shape, reinforce, and challenge these identities must be considered a relevant subject of historical research; the study of history is not confined to researching and interpreting the 'factual' past but extends to the investigation of its relevance in contemporary societies. We cognitively construct and rebuild our ideas of and attitudes towards the past by reading stories and working on problem-related tasks. But our attitudes are also changed through constant, only partially conscious confrontation with references to the past in contemporary culture. As a result, history-related play must be recognised and investigated as a form of historical learning – not as a replacement to traditional methods but as a complementary element.[2] The basis of the informal and formal educational potential of games is an understanding of historical learning as not only the acquisition of information about the past but also of how this knowledge is (co-)constructed from modern perspectives and also as a means of developing synthetic (reconstructive) and analytic (de-constructive) operations of historical thinking. One of the conditions of contemporary co-construction of historical knowledge is its 'mediality' – both in technical terms of availability of media and in terms of societal usage of these technologies.

On this basis, 'play' needs to be considered not simply as a 'purpose-free-activity' – a playful exertion of agency both within a games' structures and rules (*ludus*) and their free, uncontrolled transgression (*paidia*)[3] – but also as an activity of exploring and (re-)constructing the 'world' created through 'gameplay'. To play historical games, therefore, can be seen as an act of explorative construction of a conception of the past and of history. In this respect, the playing of historical games enables the co-construction of conceptions, beliefs, and convictions about 'the past' and its relevance is not so different from other cultural forms and media addressing history.

It is the interrelation between these different instances and media as well as process of dealing with the past which needs to be addressed when reflecting historical learning. History education as a society's institutionalised form of fostering and supervising historical learning has several tasks. It must equip students with the most valid and resilient idea of the past with which they can confront the diversity of historical statements and interpretations in contemporary culture. But it must also enable students to perceive the significance of the influence of this media on their own historical thinking. In the case of novels and films that depict and thematise the past, explicitly expressed statements have a meaning for the reception, interpretation, and historical consciousness of the recipients. But non-verbal statements and the structures of the perspective and plot can play just as strong a role in shaping this consciousness. In games, at least two aspects are added, as we will discuss in this chapter: the first is the agency of the player, their influence on the plot and on impressions of immediacy and authenticity; the second is the decisions made by the creators of these games which visibly or invisibly limit the players' possibilities of action.

Against this backdrop, neither statistical analyses of the market share of these games nor in-depth analyses of the narratives presented by these games will suffice to explain their appeal, logic, and impact. It is the activity of playing these games itself which needs to be addressed as an act of historical learning in a more complex way than just perceiving and receiving (or rejecting) the manifest or implicit narratives, values, and identities. Historical learning is much more than just transmission of 'correct' information on the interpretation of the past, the reflection about its conceptual structure and exercises in historical thinking.

As indispensable as these facets are, in our opinion the experience of one's own engagement with history-related popular media is just as important – whether privately in one's leisure time, or in exchange with others and especially the guided reflection of these experiences. To make this possible requires both empirical research into the most diverse forms of this engagement, playful co-construction of historical meaning and subsequent reflection of the same, as well as the construction of corresponding settings for history lessons. These tasks cannot be completed in the context of this chapter, but a theoretical reflection on the connection between historical playing and learning in relation to the crusades provides a useful case study which may act as a starting point for future research.

In this chapter, computer games which feature the history of the crusades are interpreted as a medium of historical culture. They stand among a number of other popular representations of this topic, including a large number of historical novels and audio-visual products. Across these media, very different treatments and different perspectives have led to the creation of very different stories,[4] and many accounts have included myths, exaggerations, and fabrications which are repeated across stories and media and, despite their questionable plausibility, contribute to popular historical conscience over time.[5] This also applies to computer games which address the history of the crusades, which, due to their special mediality and openness, allow very individual perspectives and discussions, even if the games themselves are strongly influenced by the popular narratives adopted by their creators.

Using the examples from several Grand Strategy Games which address the crusades, Robert Houghton has argued that one of the peculiarities of the medium is that the explanations of historical events are very simplified and sometimes even arbitrary. He attributes this in part to the open character of the games. At the same time, the games usually only offer the perspective of the powerful and decision-makers which greatly limits historical thinking to a narrow, personalised form. This, in combination with the restricted criteria of success in the game, leads to the occlusion of the different goals of the crusaders. Against this background, the question arises: to what extent are the games suitable for historical learning?

This chapter questions which perspectives and interpretations of the crusades, as represented within computer games, are relevant in the present. Even if the perspective of the powerful is offered, they must be attractive and relatable to the players in some way: the player must be able to identify with the protagonist, which colours the game's representation of these characters and potentially limits its usefulness as a teaching tool. Ultimately, the vast range of approaches, perspectives, and genres through which games present the crusades can provide potent support for many elements of teaching. The history of the crusades is contested and while games may provide an introduction to the historical data surrounding these events, they may act more usefully as a means to interrogate the common perceptions of these events within both the academy and more broadly in popular culture.

To this end, in this chapter we will first outline some of the key issues and tendencies embodied within modern discussion and depiction of the crusades and note that the unique nature of games creates a particular manner of approaching these issues. We will then consider the turn towards the teaching of history as a subjective competition of narratives as opposed to the more traditional 'objective' search for facts and accuracy and argue that games can facilitate this development. Finally, we will consider the potential utility of games as teaching tools for the crusades and for modern representations and perceptions of these events, highlight possible issues, and consider the importance of developing teaching through games in conjunction with traditional scholarly approaches and instruction around critical play.

## The crusades in the modern world

The crusades are a sensitive subject of history within contemporary societies. Over the last 150 years, they have become the focal point of a spectrum of historical narratives which have developed both in the European West and in the Near East, which represent, express, underpin, and reinforce different political positions and attitudes. In many Western historical narratives, the crusades stand for aristocratic and national romanticist medievalism and for the lionisation of Christian 'defence' against Muslim 'infidels'. These notions underpin far-right anti-Muslim propaganda to this day,[6] and have also served as examples of the 'criminal' nature of papal policies.[7] In recent decades, these interpretations have faded within the academy in favour of accounts of the crusades as early examples of reprehensible expansionist, colonialist, and imperialist tendencies of the West. This new approach is informed by the broader acknowledgement of the work of Islamic scholars, the emergence of postcolonialism as an intellectual field and the development of more critical stances towards the sensitive and outright negative aspects of European societies. As a result, representations of the crusades as a missed opportunity for peaceful 'intercultural encounters' and coexistence have to some extent replaced sociocentric heroic narratives even in the public sphere.[8]

In the contemporary Near East, remembering the crusades has followed a quite different development since the nineteenth century. Here, the crusades are prominent within historical narratives as the founding events of a tradition of Western intervention and injustice, and the development of a narrative in which Muslims are victims of Western aggression and economic exploitation. This narrative has played a pivotal role in anti-Western Islamic and Islamist propaganda, still in vogue among parts of the Muslim world today.[9] The sharp jihadi differentiation between Islamic societies on the one hand and 'Jahiliyyah' on the other, developed by Sayyid Qutb, underpins a differentiation not between the centuries before Muhammad and those afterwards, but between societies which follow his doctrine and those which do not.[10] As a result, where many historical narratives which follow Western temporal regimes allow the presentation of the crusades as a thing of the medieval past – overcome by modern enlightenment – for jihadist historical narratives the crusades may be conceived as an ongoing conflict. Examples of such views can be found in the writings of Osama bin Laden as well as in other Islamist texts.[11]

Of course, such observations must not reinforce a dichotomic understanding of supposed 'Western' against 'Muslim' worldviews and perspectives onto the understanding of the crusades today. In fact, these observations can highlight differentiations within these groups. Most obviously, the vast majority of Muslims are not jihadist and the vast majority of white Europeans are not members of the far-right. Outside extremist rhetoric, there are quite different interpretations of the crusades across varied historiographical traditions including the selection of timeframes, geographical areas, and religious and political context, but also, in some cases highlighting evidence of religious coexistence even at the height of the movement.[12]

These considerations can help to provide an understanding of the *possible* spectrum of perspectives and ideas within contemporary popular historical narratives around the crusades. It can be assumed that the games aim to address conventional interpretations of the crusades that are relatable to players in modern societies. At the same time, however, they not only offer historical meaning but also influence the historical consciousness within society. Within these games, the crusades are primarily characterised by being distant and alien, apt for both dreams of romantic re-enactment and flight from complexity. But these games are also for some players a highly (though sometimes maybe unconsciously so) political realm of action, the inner mechanisms of both perceiving the presented past world and of acting within it, the proto-narratives programmed into them, are of utmost importance. They include the characters' intra-game 'medieval' worldviews, but – through the act of play – relate to the players' extra-game positions, worldviews, and perspectives.

The range and contemporary significance of these historical narratives surrounding the crusades make the subject a valuable case study for the learning value of historical computer games. Not only do a substantial number of games address the crusades, but they represent multiple different perspectives. They engage with conflicting historical narratives across their audience and may consolidate or counteract the more extreme interpretations of the crusades discussed above.

## History vs. the past in education and games

History education at higher levels increasingly differentiates between 'the past' and 'history'. All perceptions and statements about societal conditions are inevitably subjective. This is the case for events of one's own time but is even more apparent when discussing past events. It is widely accepted that while 'the past' incorporated a series of concrete events, it can only be addressed from posterity through constructed accounts: what we term 'history'. Attempts to fully reconstruct the past are inevitably limited by absence of sources or incomplete accounts and by their reliance to some extent on modern frameworks. While it is certainly the case that historical reconstruction is an important element of historical study and that not all reconstructions are created equal, an overly strong focus on reconstruction may serve to conceal the role played by contemporary perspectives of events, and of current norms, values, and concepts in constructing historical narratives. This distinction between the past and history is of fundamental importance when dealing with computer games. All histories present reconstructions of the past which are subjective and open to debate, but in the case of games these reconstructions are unfinished without audience input and may be explored, interrogated, and completed through play. The question arises as to what is explicitly and implicitly understood in the games as 'crusades'? Which perspectives are represented? Who tells which story, to whom, and why?

While history education has never fully abandoned the idea of teaching and learning 'the past', it has systematically developed a focus on students' abilities to reflect on the creation of historical knowledge and the principles guiding historical insight and thinking.[13] In consequence, the phrase 'learning history' has become a broader, but also deeper, more complex concept. Learning history is no longer simply an exercise to gain factual insight into a past as it is modelled by the current state of historians' research. Historians' research still serves as a major and ineluctable point of reference but does not stand alone in presenting criteria for learning outcomes and success.

It is still sometimes argued that historical computer games may be better suited for historical learning than traditional teaching methods for their immersive qualities. This argument tacitly assumes that historical learning is equivalent to 'learning the past'. However, if a systematic distinction is made between history and the past, then this cannot be a meaningful justification for historical learning. Rather, the construction and offered meaning of historical computer games must be addressed in the context of social debates on the crusades (or other historical topics). We must consider the ways in which games construct history rather than simply looking at the

## Learning to think historically 99

narrative they provide. In this we may follow the reflections on historical learning by Jörn Rüsen. In his view, historical learning is a process whereby students simultaneously perform tasks of historical orientation, thereby progressively acquiring more complex competencies and developing the structural forms through which we express the experience and knowledge of the past.[14] For historical learning, addressing the perspective of those who participated in past events is necessary in order to identify how this data can be related to the present and how it can inform expectations for the future. The information required to construct these understandings of the past is not restricted to that obtained directly from primary sources and from scholarly literature, but can also come from fictional representations, including computer games. All these media, no matter their academic credentials, present certain interpretations to the reader or user.

Computer games occupy a unique position among popular media when it comes to the development of historical learning. There are certainly some fundamental similarities between games and other forms of media: for example, as in other media, games present one specific interpretation of the past to the player. However, unlike other media, games present their historical accounts through a more complex and flexible form characterised by player agency: the player takes a leading role in the creation of the historical account. This allows for a more complex form of engagement with the presented past. The operative process is a co-constructive engagement with the presented images of the past between the creators of the game and the player.

The fictitious character of these games does not prevent the presented concepts of a past or history from influencing the player's historical consciousness: historical fiction in any media may strongly influence a consumer's perceptions. Therefore, it is not only the accuracy or authenticity of the presentation in general which needs to be considered when reflecting on such games' contribution to historical learning, but rather the plausibility of the account considered through empirical, normative, theoretical, and narrative lenses. As Rüsen argues, we must consider which statements about the past can be supported by verifiable evidence, how these statements relate to accepted values, norms, concepts, and theories, and how the constructed patterns of meaning are disclosed, made explicit, and acceptable.[15]

However, typical play does not usually encourage players to engage with the historical accounts of games in this manner. To fully benefit from the historical learning potential of games, students must receive explicit instruction in historical thinking through both procedural and conceptual methods: they must learn how to engage in critical play. By pairing gameplay with traditional history education, students may formulate relevant historical questions and apply analytical methods as laid out in the *Förderung und Entwicklung eines reflektierten Geschichtsbewusstseins* (Promotion and Development of a Reflective Consciousness of History) group's model of historical thinking competencies.[16] Through this process they may engage in the synthetic 're-construction' of narratives about past events and conditions; and the analytical 'de-construction' of historical statements, arguments, and representations.

Both reconstructive and deconstructive operations are inherent to the play of historical games. Most situations require input from a player without the qualification provided by a traditional narrative: players must (re-)construct the inner logic of each situation, combining a range of information from different sources both from within and outside the game. In most cases, the results of these assessments are not expressed verbally or even consciously, but they represent an explicit engagement by the player with the history represented within the game. Conversely, all constructions of 'past' situations are dependent on the interpretation of history made by the game's creators, which – due to the medium's character – are seldom explicit, but rather 'coded' in both the verbal and pictorial presentation of the past world and the gameplay mechanism. These constructions are, in turn, analysed and deconstructed through the act of play. Both operations are implicit within normal play, but can also be addressed explicitly when using history games in formal educational settings, in order to foster students' respective abilities in their everyday use of computer games.

Games provide a performative form of 'living' and 'doing' history.[17] Players are active participants in the game's vision of the past. While performative forms of history outside computer games may immerse an audience into a past and allow them to act within it, these other media rely on individual and collective conceptions about the past and about feasible and non-feasible decisions. In other media, these decisions are taken primarily by the creators and are open to immediate discussion by the audience – they depend on established and known conventions. But in games this does not depend on the ability of the audience to imagine a difference between present and past, but is led by the programmers' conceptions of historical norms which are moulded into the game by programming and cannot be addressed conventionally. They must instead be addressed through critical play and in conjunction with traditional educational methods.

## Learning the crusades through play

The crusades provide a particularly useful case study for the use of historical games for educational purposes. There are a substantial range of games pertaining to this theme across almost every genre. More significantly though, these games rely on an array of popular tropes and perspectives: they represent fertile ground for the careful and supervised reconstruction of past events, but provide even more potential for the educationally profitable deconstruction of arguments and preconceptions. Games about the crusades may be useful as means to immerse students in the period, region, and events through their reconstructive elements, but they may also be used as a tool to consider the ways in which arguments and representations of the crusades are constructed and which academic and popular trends form the basis for these representations.

The immersive nature of games allows them to engage their players with the world of the crusades and provide a bridge between present and past through their active role in the reconstruction of historical events. The combination of audio-visual sceneries with the programmed interactivity within a game may produce a form of immersion which truly transgresses the boundary between past and present. The past – always dependent on abstract and cognitive re-construction – seems to become present, even if only virtually so. *Assassin's Creed* provides visually spectacular representations of Jerusalem, Damascus, and Acre. *Crusader Kings* presents a deep representation of the political factions of the Holy Land throughout the crusading period. *Medieval: Total War* renders the battlefields and troops of the conflict in vivid detail. All of this may serve to introduce the player to the crusades in a new and influential manner.

A key element of the educational potential of games about the crusades is the bi-directional interaction between intra-game learning and extra-game learning which the media can promote. In one direction, players might apply extra-game knowledge about human nature, societies, and actions in general and about the specific past events depicted in a game to support their progress within the game. For example, understanding of the significance of Jerusalem obtained from educational experience may influence player actions within the game – potentially leading to a prioritisation of capturing the city in *Crusader Kings II*. In the other direction players may integrate their intra-game experience, perceptions, and logic into an extra-game historical narrative around a specific past and about human nature across cultures and epochs. The technology tree of *Age of Empires* might not only shape players' strategy within the game, but also their extra-game perception of societal development. Games can have a substantial impact on their player's understanding of the crusades.

However, this influential power carries potential for substantial negative consequences: games may communicate outdated or intellectually and socially problematic perspectives just as effectively as they may relate material which is academically sound. Students must therefore learn to parse the history represented in games through the lens of academic scholarship. The blurring of past and present within games demands the consideration of different layers of engagement. Players may learn through an intra-game layer to identify the programmed structures of characters, their social interrelations, rules, norms, and spectrums of allowed actions and hence learn to perceive the historical narrative posed by the game. But this intra-game learning must be paired with extra-game knowledge about the period and setting of the game and an externally supported understanding of the construction of historical narratives. Players may gain an understanding of the broad complexities of the conflict through acritical play of *Assassin's Creed*, but within an educational environment this must be supported through engagement with the historiography surrounding crusade, jihad, and the broader interaction between Christianity and Islam. The modern popular origins of the game's core representations of secret medieval societies and political power must be considered alongside any medieval roots.

Students must also understand the mechanical limitations of games as media. Even though (computer) games yield a certain amount of the historian's task of sense-making to the player,[18] they also restrict it by the innate logic of their rules. This may be more obvious for strategic games which cover greater amounts of time and model historical developments, such as Sid Meier's *Civilization*, which models a concept of technological and societal progress not as the retrospectively visible outcome of a development but as a pre-defined condition of it, thus implementing a specific modern interpretation of historical development.[19] This historical determinism is visibly present within many strategy games which address the crusades. These expeditions to the Holy Land are presented as inevitable within *Medieval: Total War* and *Crusader Kings*, while the emergence of a more abstract concept of crusading is a certainty within most of the *Civilization* franchise.

Most fundamentally, students must learn to recognise that historical games represent modern images and ideologies through their constructed narratives. To engage with this, students must 'reverse-engineer' the game, not in the technical sense of getting access to the program code (although this can be of value) but by analysing the components their creators chose to emphasise, downplay, or to ignore – and the stances, postures, worldviews, values, and the knowledge which underpin these choices. For example, most games present the crusades through a primarily Western perspective. The factions of *Medieval: Total War* are primarily European, while the initial release of *Crusader Kings II* only allowed the player to select a Christian ruler. Some games, such as *Assassin's Creed* make use of a Muslim player character, but move the focus of the game away from the religious conflict to a fantasy struggle between ancient secret societies. *Age of Empires II* offers the player a campaign around the exploits of Saladin, but this is presented from the perspective of a Norman knight within Saladin's entourage.

The use of these modern ideologies extends into the logic of the gameplay: games addressing the crusades typically build political and social models based on Western perspectives and concepts of history. The scenario 'The Siege of Jerusalem' within the Saladin campaign of *Age of Empires II* requires the player to 'Continue building [their] economy and advance to the Imperial Age' as one of their objectives.[20] This objective relies on a Eurocentric framework of historical progress through a sequential ladder of ages through the Dark Age, Feudal Age, Castle Age, and finally Imperial Age. Likewise, while *Crusader Kings II* provides a substantially more detailed and considered approach to the Islamic world than many of its peers, the core of the gameplay is built on a feudal system clearly inspired by Western societies and historiography. This trend is common within games in any historical period or setting, but appears particularly pronounced when addressing the crusades.

But the flawed narratives which some of these games represent offer an important additional learning opportunity around the popular understanding of the crusades. The figures, events, and themes depicted in these games refer to interpretations and trends recognisable within popular historical narratives. Thus, the chronically ahistorical *Dante's Inferno* still has potential value as a teaching tool. The game transposes a fifteenth-century poet into a warrior on the Third Crusade and blends crusader rhetoric with the vision of hell set out within Dante's late medieval work and with modern perceptions of the Middle Ages and cynicism towards religion. As a source for the events of the crusade, the game is of negligible relevance. It is more useful for developing understanding of crusader ideology, but the main educational value of the game is as a study in modern perceptions and appropriations of the crusades alongside more general medieval tropes. In this respect, the games offer opportunities for historical learning through the critical interrogation of the narrative presented through the game world and mechanics, the acceptance or rejection of this narrative in whole or in part, and the consideration of the place of this narrative within broader modern trends.[21]

A final consequence of the interaction between intra-game and extra-game experiences of history is that the transparency of a games' logics, rules, and mechanics are of critical importance to their value as a learning tool. Games must conceal information and mechanics from their players to a certain extent: receiving too much data may render a complex game unplayable and many games rely on the player possessing only partial information as a core element of gameplay. But withholding too much information undermines a player's ability to parse the account of history set out by a game.

Ultimately, when selecting a game for teaching the crusades (or any element of history) teachers must consider a number of issues: how far does a game provide for insight into the principles and logics by which its game mechanics are constructed? How far are players aware and able to reflect on the structures which constitute the constructed past world in which they act? How far are they capable of formulating questions around the logics of actions and perceptions? How well can they identify patterns of cause and effect by efforts of trial and error? Most importantly: how far may they reflect on the meaning and consequences of the design choices around the game? Can they move beyond improving their performance within the game to consider the narratives the game offers about the past, and to the historical and political statements it makes?

In order to use historical games as educational tools students must therefore be literate in the events and historiography of the crusades, the methods through which games may communicate this history, and the modern popular influences which contribute to these representations. The games must be embedded in a programme of education which incorporates traditional approaches, but also game design and public history. This is perhaps a complex challenge, but the potential for heightened engagement and understanding of the period and its relevance in the modern world suggests that such an approach will be worthwhile.

## Conclusion

What can be taken from the discussion above? First of all, the relationship between history education and the past conditions and occurrences it addresses (in our case, the crusades) are by no means unidirectional and unifunctional, but form a complex sub-set within the diversity of contemporary historical narratives. Teaching should not merely provide knowledge about the past, against which all uses of such information within popular culture are to be measured and inevitably fail. Nor should history and its subsequent relevance only be considered as useful for understanding popular media. Likewise, it would be wrong to reduce popular media to examples and challenges by which to teach formal skills. What is needed in today's diverse and plural societies – particularly with regard to inflammatory historical issues as the crusades – is an awareness of the complex nature of history as a spectrum of contemporary constructions of narratives about a real past, their relevance and meaning for students' personal identities and the crucial role of their own critical thinking for navigating the emergent arena of engagement. History education must address this array of narratives, combining critical analyses of present media representations of the past with reflections on students' societal bearing and the importance of individual historical thinking.

Beyond this, some more concrete conclusions can be drawn for learning history with computer games:

1. Computer games addressing historical subjects are part of contemporary historical culture in that they present specific narratives about the past rooted within society's diverse reservoir of perspectives, interpretations, and evaluations of the period in question. In turn they provide new facets to this culture. In this respect, history-related computer games are not different from other popular media like books and movies. Given that there is no central control over the narratives presented and that this new kind of media has gained dominance within certain strata of society, members of society need to be able to perceive and judge these media not only in terms of the gameplay and enjoyment they offer, but also in historical terms. History education in general should explicitly aim to enable students to engage with historical games critically. History teaching in schools therefore should address the narratives they offer, not only in terms of its quality, authenticity, and reliability, but also in terms of its inner logic and appeal to particular groups.

   Such analyses should focus on the historical narratives presented within the game, the gameplay-framework which presents them and the relationship between the two: which characters and events are represented, what actions the player can take towards them. The same holds true for presence and omissions of events and actions.

2. What distinguishes computer games from other media is their fundamental interactivity, which not only offers a degree of agency in terms of game play, but also presents the need for players to apply their knowledge and concepts of the past in order to be successful. In doing so and in interacting with the gameplay-framework and the proto-narrative elements it provides, they will both use but also challenge their conceptions. History education should not be focused on enhancing gamers' chances of winning by learning historical facts, but it should make students aware of this aspect of 'historical agency' and its relationship with their own historical consciousness. In this respect,

playing history games or at least reflecting on perceptions and rationalisations associated with it, should be part of history teaching.
3   Playing a history-related computer game and reflecting on it can therefore be considered actions which imply historical thinking and therefore require historical competencies. In return, both forms of dealing with these facets of history culture can be used for fostering such competencies.

In consequence, we are concerned that games should not be considered as historical teaching tools simply for their immersive nature and value as tools of engagement. Games may certainly act in this manner, but in focusing on this quality alone we potentially undermine the utility of this media within the more complex and developed principles of historical meaning-making at higher levels of study. In the future the epistemology of historical thinking will need to be expanded beyond the opportunities and difficulties in extracting information and constructing historical narratives from different kinds of traditional sources and which differentiates between primary and retrospective secondary accounts. When addressing historical games, we must also consider the role that such secondary accounts play when the narratives they provide are determined in part by the agency-based decisions made by their consumers.

Teaching the crusades (and teaching history more generally) in the digital age cannot mean the teaching of a best availably story as the narrative against which all other representations of history across media can only be seen as distortions. Nor can it simply use such media to create vivid and detailed images and representations of the past. Instead it must work on different layers, among which enabling students to perceive and reflect on patterns and principles of the contemporary construction of the virtual worlds is of great importance.

## Notes

1 See also: Angela Schwarz, ed., *"Wollten Sie auch immer schon einmal pestverseuchte Kühe auf ihre Gegner werfen?". Eine fachwissenschaftliche Annährung an Geschichte im Computerspiel, 2* (Münster: Lit Verlag, 2012).
2 Andrew B. R. Elliott, "Simulations and Simulacra: History in Video Games," *Práticas da História* 5 (2017).
3 Roger Caillois, *Man, Play, and Games*, trans. Meyer Barash (Urbana, IL: University of Illinois Press, 2001), 20.
4 Jonathan Phillips, *The Life and Legend of the Sultan Saladin* (London: Bodley Head, 2019); Felix Hinz and Johannes Meyer-Hamme, eds., *Controversial Histories – Current Views on the Crusades: Engaging the Crusades 3* (London: Routledge, 2020).

5 Felix Hinz, *Mythos Kreuzzüge. Selbst- und Fremdbilder in historischen Romanen, 1786–2012* (Schwalbach: Wochenschau, 2014); Felix Hinz, ed., *Kreuzzüge des Mittelalters und der Neuzeit. Realhistorie – Geschichtskultur – Didaktik* (Hildesheim: Olm, 2015).
6 Michael Mannheimer, "Was uns Historiker und der Islam über die Kreuzzüge verschweigen," *Michael Mannheimer: Islamkritische Informationen – Für die Freiheit des Gedankens – Gegen jede Form von Totalitarismus* [blog], http://michael-mannheimer.info/2011/07/10/was-uns-historiker-und-der-islam-uber-die-kreuzzuge-verschweigen/, accessed September 12, 2020.
7 Prominently in: Karlheinz Deschner, *11. und 12. Jahrhundert. Von Kaiser Heinrich II., dem "Heiligen" (1002), bis zum Ende des Dritten Kreuzzugs (1192)*, 2 (Reinbek bei Hamburg: Rowohlt-Taschenbuch-Verl, 2008).
8 Michele Barricelli, "'A New, Less Tolerant Period'. Zur Darstellung der Kreuzzüge in deutschen sowie britischen, französischen und italienischen Schulgeschichtsbüchern," in *Kreuzzüge des Mittelalters und der Neuzeit. Realhistorie – Geschichtskultur – Didaktik*, ed. Felix Hinz (Hildesheim: Olms, 2015).
9 Tamim Ansary, *Destiny Disrupted: A History of the World Through Islamic Eyes* (Philadelphia: Public Affairs, 2009).
10 Musharbash, Yassin. "Wie tickt der IS?" In *Die Zeit (Online)*, March 30, 2015. http://blog.zeit.de/radikale-ansichten/2015/03/30/wie-tickt-der-1/, accessed September 12, 2020.
11 For example: "Threats and Responses; Bin Laden's Message to Muslims in Iraq: Fight the 'Crusaders'," *New York Times*, February 15, 2003, www.nytimes.com/2003/02/15/world/threats-and-responses-bin-laden-s-message-to-muslims-in-iraq-fight-the-crusaders.html, accessed September 12, 2020.
12 Missy Sullivan, "Why Muslims See the Crusades So Differently from Christians. Interview with Paul M. Cobb and Suleiman A. Mourad," in *History* (2017), www.history.com/news/why-muslims-see-the-crusades-so-differently-from-christians, accessed September 12, 2020.
13 Sam Wineburg, *Historical Thinking and Other Unnatural Acts: Charting the Future of Teaching the Past* (Philadelphia: Temple University Press, 2001); Peter Seixas and Tom Morton, *The Big Six. Historical Thinking Concepts* (Toronto: Nelson Education, 2013); Sam Wineburg, Daisy Martin, and Chauncey Monte-Sano, *Reading Like a Historian: Teaching Literacy in Middle and High School History Classrooms* (New York, NY: Teachers College Press, 2013); Michael Young and David Lambert, eds., *Knowledge and the Future School: Curriculum and Social Justice* (London: Bloomsbury, 2014).
14 Jörn Rüsen, *History. Narration, Interpretation, Orientation* (New York, NY: Berghahn Books, 2005), 36. For a criticism of Rüsen's work see: Andreas Körber, "Sinnbildungstypen als Graduierungen? Versuch einer Klärung am Beispiel der Historischen Fragekompetenz," in *Historisches Denken jetzt und in Zukunft. Wege zu einem theoretisch fundierten und evidenzbasierten Umgang mit Geschichte. Festschrift für Waltraud Schreiber zum 60 Geburtstag*, ed. Katja Lehmann, Michael Werner, and Stefanie Zabold (Berlin: Münster: Lit Verlag, 2016).
15 Jörn Rüsen, *Evidence and Meaning: A Theory of Historical Studies* (New York, NY: Berghahn Books, 2017), 38.
16 Andreas Körber, *Historical Consciousness, Historical Competencies – and beyond? Some Conceptual Development within German History Didactics*

(Fachportal Pädagogik, 2015), www.pedocs.de/volltexte/2015/10811/pdf/Koerber_2015_Development_German_History_Didactics.pdf, accessed September 12, 2020.
17 Stefanie Samida, Sarah Willner, and Georg Koch, "'Doing History' – Geschichte als Praxis. Programmatische Annäherungen," in *Doing History: Performative Praktiken in der Geschichtskultur*, ed. Sarah Willner, Georg Koch, and Stefanie Samida (Münster: Waxmann, 2020).
18 Adam Chapman, "Affording History: Civilization and the Ecological Approach," in *Playing with the Past: Digital Games and the Simulation of History*, ed. Matthew Kappell and Andrew B. R. Elliott (New York, NY, 2013), 64–66.
19 M. Cecalupo and E. Chiarantoni, *Neolítico: Quando gli uomini avevano soltanto le mani e l'intelligenza, e inventarono le città* (Molfetta: la meridiana, 1996); A. Rothenhäusler, "Der Technologiebaum als Reproduktionsort wissenschaftlich-technischer Narrative," in *Paidia. Zeitschrift für Computerspielforschung* (2017), www.paidia.de/der-technologiebaum-als-reproduktionsort-wissenschaftlich-technischer-narrative/, accessed July 16, 2020.
20 "The Siege of Jerusalem," in *Age of Empires Series Wiki*, https://ageofempires.fandom.com/wiki/The_Siege_of_Jerusalem, accessed August 26, 2020.
21 Johannes Meyer-Hamme, "Was heißt 'historisches Lernen?' Eine Begriffsbestimmung im Spannungsfeld gesellschaftlicher Anforderungen, subjektiver Bedeutungszuschreibungen und Kompetenzen historischen Denkens," in *Geschichtsunterricht im 21. Jahrhundert. Eine geschichtsdidaktische Standortbestimmung*, ed. Thomas Sandkühler, Charlotte Bühl-Gramer, Anke John, and Astrid Schwabe (Göttingen: V & R Unipress, 2018), 75–92.

## Bibliography

Ansary, Tamim. *Destiny Disrupted: A History of the World Through Islamic Eyes*. Philadelphia: Public Affairs, 2009.

Barricelli, Michele. "'A New, Less Tolerant Period.' Zur Darstellung der Kreuzzüge in deutschen sowie britischen, französischen und italienischen Schulgeschichtsbüchern." In *Kreuzzüge des Mittelalters und der Neuzeit. Realhistorie – Geschichtskultur – Didaktik*, edited by Felix Hinz, 237–54. Hildesheim: Olms, 2015.

Caillois, Roger. *Man, Play, and Games*, translated by Meyer Barash. Urbana, IL: University of Illinois Press, 2001.

Cecalupo, M., and E. Chiarantoni. *Neolítico: Quando gli uomini avevano soltanto le mani e l'intelligenza, e inventarono le città*. Molfetta: la meridiana, 1996.

Chapman, Adam. "Affording History: Civilization and the Ecological Approach." In *Playing with the Past: Digital Games and the Simulation of History*, edited by Matthew Kappell and Andrew B. R. Elliott, 61–73. New York, NY: Bloomsbury, 2013.

Deschner, Karlheinz. *11. und 12. Jahrhundert. Von Kaiser Heinrich II., dem "Heiligen" (1002), bis zum Ende des Dritten Kreuzzugs (1192)*. 2. Reinbek bei Hamburg: Rowohlt-Taschenbuch-Verl, 2008.

Elliott, Andrew B. R. "Simulations and Simulacra: History in Video Games." *Práticas da História* 5 (2017): 11–41.

Hinz, Felix, ed. *Kreuzzüge des Mittelalters und der Neuzeit. Realhistorie – Geschichtskultur – Didaktik*. Hildesheim: Olm, 2015.

———. *Mythos Kreuzzüge. Selbst- und Fremdbilder in historischen Romanen, 1786–2012*. Schwalbach: Wochenschau, 2014.

Hinz, Felix, and Meyer-Hamme Johannes, eds. *Controversial Histories – Current Views on the Crusades: Engaging the Crusades 3*. London: Routledge, 2020.

Körber, Andreas. *Historical Consciousness, Historical Competencies – and Beyond? Some Conceptual Development within German History Didactics*. Fachportal Pädagogik, 2015. www.pedocs.de/volltexte/2015/10811/pdf/Koerber_2015_Development_German_History_Didactics.pdf. Accessed September 12, 2020.

———. "Sinnbildungstypen als Graduierungen? Versuch einer Klärung am Beispiel der Historischen Fragekompetenz." In *Historisches Denken jetzt und in Zukunft. Wege zu einem theoretisch fundierten und evidenzbasierten Umgang mit Geschichte. Festschrift für Waltraud Schreiber zum 60 Geburtstag*, edited by Katja Lehmann, Michael Werner, and Stefanie Zabold, 27–41. Berlin: Münster: Lit Verlag, 2016.

Mannheimer, Michael. "Was uns Historiker und der Islam über die Kreuzzüge verschweigen." *Michael Mannheimer: Islamkritische Informationen – Für die Freiheit des Gedankens – Gegen jede Form von Totalitarismus* [blog]. http://michael-mannheimer.info/2011/07/10/was-uns-historiker-und-der-islam-uber-die-kreuzzuge-verschweigen/. Accessed September 12, 2020.

Meyer-Hamme, Johannes. "Was heißt 'historisches Lernen'? Eine Begriffsbestimmung im Spannungsfeld gesellschaftlicher Anforderungen, subjektiver Bedeutungszuschreibungen und Kompetenzen historischen Denkens." In *Geschichtsunterricht im 21. Jahrhundert. Eine geschichtsdidaktische Standortbestimmung*, edited by Thomas Sandkühler, Charlotte Bühl-Gramer, Anke John, and Astrid Schwabe, 75–92. Göttingen: V & R Unipress, 2018.

Musharbash, Yassin. "Wie tickt der IS?" *Die Zeit (Online)*, March 30, 2015. http://blog.zeit.de/radikale-ansichten/2015/03/30/wie-tickt-der-1/. Accessed September 12, 2020.

Phillips, Jonathan. *The Life and Legend of the Sultan Saladin*. London: Bodley Head, 2019.

Rothenhäusler, A. "Der Technologiebaum als Reproduktionsort wissenschaftlich-technischer Narrative." In *Paidia. Zeitschrift für Computerspielforschung* (2017). www.paidia.de/der-technologiebaum-als-reproduktionsort-wissenschaftlich-technischer-narrative/. Accessed July 16, 2020.

Rüsen, Jörn. *Evidence and Meaning. A Theory of Historical Studies*. New York, NY: Berghahn Books, 2017.

———. *History. Narration, Interpretation, Orientation*. New York, NY: Berghahn Books, 2005.

Samida, Stefanie, Willner Sarah, and Koch Georg. " 'Doing History' – Geschichte als Praxis. Programmatische Annäherungen." In *Doing History. Performative Praktiken in der Geschichtskultur*, edited by Sarah Willner, Georg Koch, and Stefanie Samida, 1–25. Münster, New York, NY: Waxmann, 2020.

Schwarz, Angela, ed. *"Wollten Sie auch immer schon einmal pestverseuchte Kühe auf ihre Gegner werfen?" Eine fachwissenschaftliche Annährung an Geschichte im Computerspiel*, 2. Münster: LIT-Verlag, 2012.

Seixas, Peter, and Morton Tom. *The Big Six. Historical Thinking Concepts*. Toronto: Nelson Education, 2013.

Sullivan, Missy. "Why Muslims See the Crusades So Differently from Christians. Interview with Paul M. Cobb and Suleiman A. Mourad." In *History* (2017). www.history.com/news/why-muslims-see-the-crusades-so-differently-from-christians Accessed September 12, 2020.

"The Siege of Jerusalem." In *Age of Empires Series Wiki*. https://ageofempires.fandom.com/wiki/The_Siege_of_Jerusalem. Accessed August 26, 2020.

"Threats and Responses; Bin Laden's Message to Muslims in Iraq: Fight the 'Crusaders'." *New York Times*, February 15, 2003. www.nytimes.com/2003/02/15/world/threats-and-responses-bin-laden-s-message-to-muslims-in-iraq-fight-the-crusaders.html. Accessed September 12, 2020.

Wineburg, Sam. *Historical Thinking and Other Unnatural Acts: Charting the Future of Teaching the Past*. Philadelphia: Temple University Press, 2001.

Wineburg, Sam, Martin Daisy, and Monte-Sano Chauncey. *Reading Like a Historian: Teaching Literacy in Middle and High School History Classrooms*. New York, NY: Teachers College Press, 2013.

Young, Michael, and Lambert David, eds. *Knowledge and the Future School: Curriculum and Social Justice*. London: Bloomsbury, 2014.

# Index

9/11 attacks 18, 64–5

*Age of Empires/Age of Empires II* 1, 101, 103
*Alamut* 57, 59
Aligheri, Dante 30
*Anno 1404* 93
*The Assassins. A Radical Sect in Islam* 65
*Assassin's Creed* 1, 3, 37, 93, 101, 102–3; Altaïr Ibn-La'ahad and Al-Mualim in 60–2; environment in 62–4; Ismaili Nizaris and the Assassins in 56–8; media references to, following 9/11 64–5; non-player characters in 62–3; 'Nothing is true, everything is permitted' in 59–60; plotline of 53–6
Ayo, D. A. 31

Bartol, V. 57, 59
*Battlefleet Gothic* 13, 21
Bogost, I. 2
*Bram Stoker's Dracula* 35

Chadwick, O. 31
Chirilă, O.-A. 4
*Civilization* and *Civilization II* 1, 71, 82–3, 102; causes of the crusades in 73–6; objectives of the crusades in 79–80; participants in the crusades in 76–8
Cobb, P. 55
Constable, G. 72
Coppola, F. F. 35

Corbin, H. 59
*Crusader Kings I* and *II* 1, 3; causes of the crusades in 73–6; learning the crusades through 101–3; participants in the crusades in 78
crusades and crusaders: in *Assassin's Creed* 56–64; causes of the 73–6; in *Dante's Inferno* 32–7; in *Holy Fury* 80–3; 'leap of faith' and 57–8; learned through play 100–4; masculinities of 31–2, 40–4; massacre at Acre and 37–40; misrepresentations in strategy games 71–83; in the modern world 96–7; objectives of the 78–80; participants in the 76–8; as source material for digital games 1–4; in *Star Trek* 12, 16–18; in *Star Wars* 12, 13–16; in *Warhammer 40,000* 13, 18–21

*Dante's Inferno* 3, 30–2, 44–6, 103; adapting medieval and crusader masculinities 40–4; crusading tropes in 32–7; massacre at Acre in 37–40
Desilets, S. 34, 60
*Diablo III* 1
*Dungeons and Dragons* 1

*Elder Scrolls Online* 1
Elliott, A. B. R. 30, 34
Essary, B. K. 31

*Final Fantasy* 1
Flügel, G. 58, 59
*Förderung und Entwicklung eines reflektierten Geschichtsbewusstseins*

(Promotion and Development of a Reflective Consciousness of History) 100

games, digital: conclusions on learning history through 104–6; the crusades as source material for 1–4; Grand Strategy 71–83; history vs. the past in education and 98–100; for learning the crusades through play 100–4; non-player characters in 62–3; as performative form of 'living' and 'doing' history 100; popular culture and 12; potential as historical learning and communication tools 2–3; reconstructive and deconstructive 100; teaching of history in 93–6
*God of War* 31
Grand Strategy Games 71–3, 81–3; causes of the crusades in 73–6; *Holy Fury* 80–1; objectives of the crusades in 78–80; participants in the crusades in 76–8

history vs. the past in education and games 98–100
*Holy Fury* 80–3
Horswell, M. 30, 34
Houghton, R. 4

*Inferno* 30–1, 35, 43

Jotischky, A. 79

*Kingdom of Heaven* 36
Knight, J. 30, 34, 35, 37
Konzack, L. 54
Körber, A. 4

Lambros, J. 34
*Legacy of Kain* 1
Lewis, K. J. 4
*Lionheart: Legacy of the Crusader* 1
Lucasfilm 13

masculinities 31–2, 34, 40–4
massacre at Acre 37–40
*Medieval: Total War* 1, 71, 72, 101, 102; causes of the crusades in 73–6; objectives of the crusades in 79–80; participants in the crusades in 76–8

Meier, S. 102
Meyer-Hamme, J. 4
*Mount and Blade* 83

Nicolle, D. 55
Nietzsche, F. 59

Okrand, M. 16
orientalism 55

*Paradox Interactive* 83
*Pilgrim: Faith as a Weapon* 93
popular culture 12
Purkis, W. 33–4

*Qur'an* 57
Qutb, S. 96–7

*Reigns* 83
*Resident Evil* 12
*Robin and Marian* 37, 38
*Robin Hood* 37, 38
*Robin Hood: Prince of Thieves* 37
Roddenberry, G. 16
Rüsen. J. 99

Said, E. 55
Schoen, L. M. 17
Scott, R. 36, 38
Scott, W. 37
Spencer, S. J. 38
*Star Trek* 12, 16–18
*Star Wars* 12, 13–16
*Stronghold: Crusader* 1, 93

*Talisman, The* 37
terrorism 18, 64–5
Tyerman, C. 72

Ubisoft 53

Veugen, C. 65
von Hammer, J. 58
von Lübeck, A. 57

*Warhammer 40,000* 13, 18–21
'War on Terror' 65
Wenskaus, R. 4
*World of Warcraft* 1

For Product Safety Concerns and Information please contact our EU representative GPSR@taylorandfrancis.com
Taylor & Francis Verlag GmbH, Kaufingerstraße 24, 80331 München, Germany

www.ingramcontent.com/pod-product-compliance
Lightning Source LLC
Chambersburg PA
CBHW051755230426
43670CB00012B/2294